T0024185

THANK GOD FOR Cats!

How God Speaks to Us through Our Feline Furbabies

LINDA S. CLARE

ILLUSTRATED BY Sandy Silverthorne

BroadStreet
PUBLISHING

BroadStreet Publishing® Group, LLC
Savage, Minnesota, USA
BroadStreetPublishing.com

Thank God for Cats!: How God Speaks to Us through Our Feline
Furbabies

9781424565498 (faux leather)
9781424565504 (ebook)

Stock or custom editions of BroadStreet Publishing titles may be
purchased in bulk for educational, business, ministry, fundraising,
or sales promotional use. For information, please email
orders@broadstreetpublishing.com.

Represented by Nick Harrison with Wordserve Literary.

Cover and interior by Garborg Design Works | garborgdesign.com

Printed in China

23 24 25 26 27 5 4 3 2 1

DEDICATION

From Linda

To Paladine, Oliver, Melchior, Xena Warrior Kitty, Frances, Mamma Mia!, and my family, who forever inspire me to thank God for cats.

From Sandy

To Vicki, my wife, best friend, and greatest cheerleader. Thank you for encouraging me to do this drawing thing.

To Christy. I love your sense of humor, creativity, and ability to connect people. You're the best.

And to Gracie, our tuxedo cat who loves to get up on my desk and get between me and what I'm supposed to be working on. Good kitty.

TABLE OF CAT-TENTS

Introduction

HAVE YOU THANKED A CAT LATELY?

[G]ive thanks in all circumstances;
for this is God's will for you in Christ Jesus.

1 THESSALONIANS 5:18 NIV

When my family recently gifted me with an official Cat Person Starter Kit, consisting of a middle-aged female action figure and about a dozen little plastic cats, I was thrilled.

It's so true and so *me*. I've lost count of how many cats I've fed, rescued, or adopted. But I've never *owned* any of them. Aficionados know you don't have cats—they have *you*.

Cats of all colors, sizes, and temperaments own us: black, white, gray, ginger ones; calicos, shorthairs, longhairs, petite cats; hunky, chunky ones; the striped or spotted or tuxedoed; and the three-legged and special needs kitties find loving humans.

Whether they have magnificent, plumed tails or no tails, cats of all stripes, patterns, and sizes seem to find us to express affection and demand extra treats. They must sense we love them too—around dinnertime, cats always weave around and through their people's legs.

Stereotypes abound: cats are aloof creatures that don't care about us or anything else that doesn't benefit them. But genuine cat people know that's not true: we form deep and lasting bonds with the four-pawed friends God gives us. Whether we need companionship or comfort, cats are ready to help. Especially if there's something in it for them.

Although we love to laugh at feline foibles and faux paws, cats seem to know when we're sick or lonely or just in need of some extra head bumps. In the midst of our long dark nights of the soul, our cats come to the rescue. Long, loud purrs from a kitty curled up on our laps make things better for everyone.

Cat lovers everywhere have favorite stories of the cats in their lives. From strays, ferals, and rescues to purebred divas and high-priced show cats, cats are experts at working their way into our hearts, convincing us that we can't live without them.

Felis catus, the common housecat, shows us God at work in our lives. Sure, kitties often demand breakfast well before dawn and never seem to know if they want in or out. But cats also comfort and console, showing us God's way to faith, renewed hope, and love. We can be thankful for cats, who celebrate the Creator with meows, tail flicks, and kneaded biscuits. Celebrate cats long enough and loud enough, and someday you, too, may qualify for a Cat Person Starter Kit.

Chapter 1

WHY GOD MADE CATS

*I praise you because I am
fearfully and wonderfully made;
your works are wonderful,
I know that full well.*

PSALM 139:14 NIV

Have you ever wondered why God made cats? Picture poor Noah, trying to get all the animals safely inside the ark. Just as God tells Noah, "The water's rising, so bar the door," at least one cat immediately needs to go out. Again.

Okay, make up your mind. In or out.

Or maybe one of the pair has dillydallied so long that he's sopping wet by the time he gets back inside the ark. We all know that a soaking wet cat is likely muttering more swear words than your average parrot. With his fur slicked down, he looks like a grumpy human in his birthday suit, but his attitude is quite catty. God must have rolled his eyes with all that caterwauling.

After forty days and forty nights of nonstop rain, Noah sent out the dove to find dry land. The dove brought back an olive branch, but the cats weren't impressed. One was overheard complaining, "That bird should've brought back catnip."

By the time civilization got started again, the Egyptians had enslaved the Israelites and worshiped cats. All through history, although their main job was mouse patrol, cats meowed their way into our homes and into our hearts.

Cat people love the kitties that choose them, and we're thankful for their many attributes.

But do we know a cat's inner workings? What makes a cat tick?

Awesome Anatomy

The good Lord surely knew that *felis catus* would be a huge hit. Cats' senses and abilities seem almost magical—flexible spines make it possible for them to fall from high places yet somehow land on their feet.

Cats have 230 bones—humans only have 206. Many of these extra bones are vertebrae: thirty bones of the neck and spine, plus twenty or so caudal, or tail, bones (except in the Manx). These additional spinal bones allow cats much more flexibility than humans have. That's why cats can twist into pretzels and still sleep comfortably.

Cats who happen to jump or fall from high places can twist and right themselves, adding to the myth that cats always land on their feet. In reality, cats don't always land on their feet—some seem as clumsy as humans as they plummet. But with the additional spinal vertebrae and the added stability of their tails, most cats have a much better chance than their humans of landing safely and then calmly walking away.

Cats are digitigrades, meaning that they walk on their toes. Try walking on your toes—you'll quickly learn why God didn't make you a ballerina or a cat. Plus, cats' claws, besides being deadly weapons when they climb your pantleg, are protractible. They have to *decide* to unsheathe those murder weapons on your favorite drapes.

Another Creator masterstroke: cats' shoulders are free-floating—they're able to pass through any opening that their heads will fit. The good Lord may have known humans would love shooting videos of kitties with their heads stuck in the tissue box. Many

a chonky kitty has gotten his hind end stuck in an opening that his head fit through.

Their skulls are unusual in the animal kingdom, too, with large eye sockets and jaws specially aligned for small prey such as mice. Or that hunk of chicken on your plate. When you scold your cat, those over-sized eyes immediately give you their best persecuted look to make you feel like a heel.

In the darkest night, a cat can see a mouse running in tall grass. Those reflective, spooky eyes are God's version of night vision.

So why do so many cats miss their target when jumping from the bed to the shelf? It's a mystery even spookier in the night when their eyes reflect like giant alien lasers.

And the ears! Thirty-two muscles swivel cat ears 180 degrees, and each ear moves independently. It's cat radar. This is why you can't sneak into your kitchen for a snack without attracting cats from every corner of the house. In the olden days, all cats knew the sound of a can opener and came a-running.

I thought you were asleep.

Nowadays, the reason cat food companies make pull tabs on their cans is to give humans a two-second head start.

Part of our attraction to cats is how awesome God made them, and for centuries humans have tried to emulate them. We try to become stealthy as cats, canny as cat burglars, and quiet as kittens in a quest to be less clumsy or, in some cases, less bull-in-china-shop destructive. Unfortunately, we can't see in the dark, swivel our ears, or fit in any space our heads fit through, although some people have had their hands caught in the cookie jar.

Our Cat Teachers

Our feline furbabies can teach us so much about living. If we pay attention, we see God working through our kitties to help us be more compassionate, show more kindness, grow our hearts to hold more love even after we've pounced on one another or swiped at inanimate objects.

We can practice how cats sense when we're feeling down and go curl up next to a lonely friend. Most friends, however, would prefer you not camp out directly on their heads. We can appreciate the head bumps they give us and show kindness to strangers, but if you try to groom a stranger, you'll get a rude awakening. The loyalty and steadfast love our cats show can spur us to love God and our neighbor more and more—hopefully, without too much shed fur.

Back on the ark, Noah surely was relieved on the day all the animals streamed back onto dry land. Cooped up inside for about a year would drive anyone crazy. But the cats, true to their nature, stood at the ark's door for hours, debating whether it was best to go out or stay in. At last, Noah must have given their little patooties a gentle shove. Then the kitties spent the rest of the day grooming and basking under the rainbow of God's promises, soaking up the sun, purring as loudly as possible.

The fact that cats purr is perhaps the most mysterious quality of all God's creatures. Did you know that cats can either roar or purr but not both? Most of us prefer purrs, hands down. Our house cats' purrs bring down blood pressure and elevate our moods. We could do worse than to imitate them. Of course, most of us don't purr as often as we should.

But that's why God made cats.

Why God Made Humans

Ask any cat why God made people, and he'll likely answer that cats needed someone to open the cans of tuna. Of course, felines are prone to see themselves as the center of the universe. Now and then, it's a good idea to remind our privileged pets that God created mankind in his own image and called us "very good."

These days, more and more people feel worried, anxious, and lonely. We're unsure about the future as waves of calamity hit us more often than we can remember. It's natural to hunker down, circle the wagons, and guard our hearts against hurt and rejection. But God says, "Do not be anxious about anything, but in every situation, by prayer and petition,

with thanksgiving, present your requests to God"
(Philippians 4:6 NIV).

Cats seem to sense that God created us not for
anxiety but to love and be loved. Still, as any good
barn cat knows, you can't catch mice without the
chase. Rewards don't often come without risk. Only as
we risk our hearts to love God and love one another
do we find a peace that transcends all understanding
(v. 7). Then, along the way, we might find a sunny spot
to rest our cares.

When cats mysteriously rise up and appear on
our doorsteps at lonely times, they may appear needy.

But while we love them into trusting us, a
strong, invisible bond forms as they love us back. We
tell ourselves we chose our cat companions when
we know deep down that they've chosen us. And in

the same way, we can choose God. As Psalm 119:30 reminds us, "I have chosen the way of faithfulness; I have set my heart on your laws" (NIV).

If you've ever been ill and your cat wouldn't leave your side until you felt better, you've received real love. If you've taken in a sick kitten or fed a feral, you've freely given love away. Cats don't always show it, but they love their humans and are deeply loyal.

Eleven-year-old Jingles is Kris Brown's faithful Ragdoll who helped watch over Kris' mom, who had Parkinson's. Jingles meowed loudly to wake Mom if she slept too long and amused her with antics. When Mom passed away, Jingles became listless and sad. Then Kris herself became very ill. Jingles' spark came back, and she perked up to care for Kris as she once had for her mom. Kris is better now, but Jingles still provides daily laughter, companionship, and oodles of snuggles. Kris will always be thankful for Jingles, a caregiver cat if ever there was one.

God approves of those who seek out the lonely, oppressed, or overlooked. Again and again, Scripture admonishes us to care for the widows and orphans, the needy and the disadvantaged. Watch closely and you'll see how our cats love us unconditionally. We humans could do worse than to imitate our furry friends as they love us into giving over our half of the bed.

Prayer

Lord, help me to remember that when I'm anxious, you take me into your arms, smooth out my ruffled fur, and offer your peace that passes understanding.

Paws-itive Faith Steps

- Give your cat(s) extra chin scritches and tell them how much you love them.
- Tell your family the same but swap chin scritches for hugs.
- Practice thankfulness, even if it's only that the cat barf missed the rug today.

Chapter 2

THE AWW FACTOR:
KITTENS AND CUTENESS

*Like newborn babies, crave pure spiritual milk,
so that by it you may grow up in your salvation.*

1 PETER 2:2 NIV

Who can resist a tiny kitten? Even non-cat people find it tough to say no to a fluffy little fur ball who climbs up your pantleg and mews in your ear—the very picture of innocence. If you want to soften up a grouch or convince him to buy whatever you're selling, get a kitten. Next thing you know, the grouch will name the critter and then spend serious money on cat toys.

Got you a few cat toys.

Cat babies are blind and deaf at birth, making them super vulnerable. While there's no evidence that Jesus ever had pets, it's not hard to imagine that he'd start with a kitten or two. From the mama cat who lovingly cares for her babies to the courage of a six-week-old kitten tackling a monster ball of yarn, kittens are a perfect illustration of God's love.

Who hasn't felt God carrying them by the neck fur when they've strayed a little too far from the barn? Or felt the warmth of God's comfort when loneliness or calamity pushes them to the edge of safety? And if we, like kittens, have chased that laser dot until we're exhausted, God bids us to curl up next to him and rest.

Cat rescuer Hester Douglas wondered whether restarting her organization was a good move as she recovered from a dual liver and kidney organ transplant. She'd waited a long time for her life-saving surgery and now tried to focus on healing. But Salvada and Annie couldn't wait. The tiny orphans needed around-the-clock bottle feeding to survive, and Hester rose to the challenge. With Sali and Annie's help, Hester plans to reopen Stormy Acres Pet Rescue so she can rescue more pets in need. She's thankful for these two kittens who helped put Hester's heart back in the right place.

Although humans aren't born deaf and blind, human moms, like mama cats, bond with their young ones early on. Moms of every type recognize their child's unique smells, cries, and physical features from the moment they first meet their newborn.

Kittens begin to show their personalities early on—some elbow into the milk bar, others are shy. As they grow, kittens and babies get all sorts of education from their moms: How to bat at Mom's tail. How to sit at the treat spot and look cute. How far a kitten or a kid can push Mom before she runs out of patience.

Smart kitties learn exactly how to ambush their siblings, wrestle them to the ground, and then scamper away. They become daring, stalking imaginary prey as they high-step through tall grass.

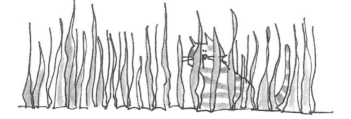

Exploring God's great big, beautiful world, they marvel at things they see for the first time. And like their human counterparts, if they stray a bit too far, they cry loudly for rescue. Kids and kittens and God's children often think they know everything until trouble strikes. Then they're mewing like mad until a gracious God bails them out. Again. Why? God thinks we're all just so darn cute.

Photo Ops Tops

That cuteness factor helps kittens play right into the human's hands. To say a kitten is photogenic is an understatement. Ask any cat. They think we invented cameras so people wouldn't get bored on the internet.

If the humans can manage to move the napping kitten from the keyboard, a whole world of cute kitten pics and videos provide hours of viewing pleasure (also known as wasting time) to humans who really do have better things to do. But don't close that browser window too fast. We can learn so many lessons from these pint-sized posers. Think about it—kittens showcase God's urgings to love more deeply, to care for others with compassion, to be there for the least of these, and to melt hearts when they've hardened from too much bad news.

Popular kitten pix and videos include kittens with horrible injuries whose rescuers nursed them to health. One video shows the story of a tiny, abandoned kitten that follows a dog home, where the dog's owners feed and care for the kitten. Kittens rescued from storm drains, tangled in fishing line, or just on the verge of starvation help us remember God's commandments to be kind and merciful.

If you're not online, never fear. Kittens are featured on calendars and greeting cards, all with young cats looking out at you with soulful kitten eyes or engaged in kittenish play. These, too, can remind us that our hearts must stay soft and pliable to allow God to work in us.

And what could be more satisfying than snapping photos of babies? The "aww" factor that kittens possess has melted many a heart while their human companions try to get the perfect pic. Kittens grow up quickly, and that cuteness factor won't last—especially after the first time your teen kitty borrows your favorite shirt to shed fur on. It's important to shoot plenty of photos of innocent kittens before you start feeling triggered by their rebellions.

The thousands of photos on your phone will help you remember how cute your kitten was, now that he weighs twenty pounds and sleeps twenty-three hours a day. Yesterday, his chunkiness got him stuck in the cat flap, but once upon a time, your fat cat was this teensy creature you held in the palm of your hand. Think about that the next time you happen to step in something gushy on your way to the kitchen. A cat's baby pictures might replace the urge for you to put him in time-out, remembering how God often doles out mercy and grace to us.

Just Add Kittens

Kittens just want to have fun. They can chase, pounce, and release a scrap of paper the same way they'd do serious damage to a field mouse. As they learn how to be cats—goofing off, playing with a string and feather, rassling their sibs—we get to watch them having a good time.

What could be more hilarious than a kitten who thinks the family dog's tail is wagging so Kitty can practice his attack strategy? Or a tiny calico batting at a man's beard? A herd of kittens clinging to a guy's pantleg? Kittens' habits of getting into things they can't easily get out of (such as a shopping bag or a flower vase) provide endless entertainment and chuckles when life gets too hard.

When you're having a bad day and can't quite see God's hand in it, kittens have a simple solution. Set an empty box on the floor or wiggle a shoelace. Kittens can't resist the invitation to lighten things up. They can move our trauma needles from red-zone terrible to yellow-zone slightly less terrible as we watch them pounce and miss and pounce again.

Situations that normally frustrate or anger us can feel almost comical when we add kittens. If you don't believe it, try changing bed sheets with a fun-loving, playful youngster. The little rascal will dive at puckers and slide on flat sheets as if he were on skis. And not the bunny slope either.

Before you know it, a kitten who is trying to conquer Mont Blanc Sheet will lighten your emotional load. Maybe God made kittens not just to be cute. Maybe they're meant to give us stress relief, to help us remember to pray for divine assistance, and, failing that, to add a bit of fun to life. What's a wrinkly sheet compared to a kitten who's having a ball?

Maybe God knows that no matter how upset and discouraged we get, life is better if we rely on his love and mercy to carry us through it. And when we forget, kittens will be there to remind us to laugh, love, and never let a good toy mouse go to waste. Before we throw up our hands and declare that all is lost, just add kittens and watch what God can do.

All in God's Family

Kittens learn their place in the litter even before their eyes are open. To get a decent breakfast, a kitten often must fight to get a place at the table, but after everyone is milk-drunk, it's all fun and games. In human families, the same is often true—except that in too many families, it's hard to feel as if you really belong.

Thankfully, in God's family we are all loved unconditionally. As the book of Isaiah says, "I will be your God through all your lifetime, yes, even when your hair is white with age. I made you and I will care for you. I will carry you along and be your Savior" (Isaiah 46:4 TLB). If you're one of those who feel like the black cat in the family, you can rest assured that God will never stop loving you. The same Creator who puts cute toe beans on kittens also thinks you're pretty special too.

GOD LOVES the BLACK CATS of the family

We who love cats know we belong to a special club. Its kitty members follow us home, appear on our doorsteps, and come to us for help. The humans in the club also have much to bond over. Who doesn't want to assign silly captions to cat pics or talk endlessly about their feline's feats and foibles?

Cat lovers everywhere can band together to deflect all those baseless stories about cats running their lives. When our kitties amuse us, we laugh together until tears run down our cheeks and our sides ache. When we catch cats being cute, we can sing out a unanimous "aww." And when a cat lover must say goodbye to a precious cat companion, we can all cry together in sympathy.

Women of a certain age are often jokingly called cat ladies. And why not? By the time you climbed over the hill, many of your friends and family are gone. Cats can fill a void like few other creatures, head bumping and kneading the lonely right out of you. When you belong to a cat club, you're too busy trying to keep your sofa arms from being shredded to be lonely. A cat who sleeps on your head is only showing you that you belong.

God probably won't sleep on your head, but God will never leave or forsake you either. Over and over in Scripture, we're admonished not to fear. The reason? God loves his children even more than we love a magnificent tuxedo named Frank. Plus, God will never sit on your crossword puzzle.

And even if your human family deserts you in your time of need, in God's family you'll never be a stranger. Plus, if you get lonely, God has a perfect remedy: just get yourself a cat or three. They'll keep you warm as they take over your bed, and they'll purr for hours on end. And every time you come home, you'll be greeted with joyous meows followed by meows that roughly translate, "Feed me. Now!" After all, they say home is the place where they have to let you in—or out—or in.

Prayer

Lord, when the world seems as if it's falling apart, I admit that I worry. Help me take to heart your admonition not to worry and keep me smiling. If necessary, send me some kittens.

Paws-itive Faith Steps

- When it's hot outside, keep a pan of fresh water where a thirsty cat or dog can get to it.
- When it's cold or snowy or rainy, construct a

makeshift shelter for strays to stay warm. A plastic bin turned on its side, lined with a towel or blanket, works well.

- Allow someone with only a few items to cut in front of you in the supermarket line. If they're buying cat food, make small talk about cats.

Chapter 3

THE AARGH FACTOR: HAIRBALLS AND OTHER GIFTS

Do not remember the sins of my youth and my rebellious ways; according to your love remember me, for you, LORD, are good.

PSALM 25:7 NIV

The minute we fall in love with a kitten's ultimate cuteness, it happens. Our little bundle of fur grows and becomes a teenager kitty. It's that awkward stage: not quite old enough to nap all day but still young enough to get away with the occasional stroll on a kitchen counter.

Teen kitties have something to prove, all right. If teen cats could drive, let's just say they'd bring home Dad's minivan with the gas gauge on empty and a dent in the fender.

Thankfully, teen cats don't drive, but that doesn't stop them from typical teenage reactions. That cute kitten's plaintive mew has deepened to an irritating meow and must be practiced as loudly as possible at three in the morning. The kitten who followed you everywhere now sulks and refuses to move when you try to make the bed.

Your teen cat will rebel, turning up his nose at food he loved last week. No matter how often you change the brand or how much it costs, teen cat makes a gagging motion before shaking his paw and walking away. Some teen cats even go on hunger strikes. These cats hold out for more wet food, and when you finally cave and serve him the fanciest feast you can buy, he gags dramatically and barfs it onto the best rug in the house.

Nope.

Some teen cats instinctively know that soon, very soon, they will go through a coming-of-age ritual that will change them forever. Their trip to the vet for a *little operation* tames the primal urges all teenagers must face, thereby keeping population growth in check. After this insult, your teen cat won't be cattin' around anymore. But by taking the tom out of tomcat, a young adult kitty is now free to work on other important feline skills.

How to Cat

Although some adult cats and people never stop acting like teenagers, most kitties take adulthood seriously. This is the stage where what your mom taught you early on really matters. All cats must master things like proper tongue baths, prime places to hock a hairball, and how to appear graceful even though, technically, you didn't land on your feet.

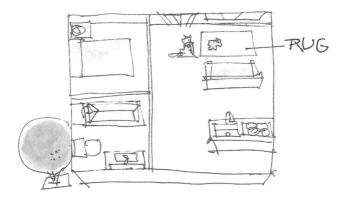

When we start on our faith journey, we also must first learn to walk then run. As 1 Corinthians 13:11 tells us, "When I was a child, I talked like a child, I thought like a child, I reasoned like a child. When I became a man, I put the ways of childhood behind me" (NIV). But along the adolescent path, our spiritual growth can zigzag like a cat picking her way through tall grass. God must smile as we tumble and stumble, straying off the path. Then God picks us up and gently sets us back on the road, perhaps with a reminder to keep our eyes on the Lord and stop climbing the drapes.

A teen cat must also perfect purring, kneading, head bumping, and leg rubbing. A few cats will try their paws at diving for a human's feet as she walks and advanced serpentine weaving, in, out, and around their person's legs. A more adventurous feline will scale her human's backside, supervising from atop a shoulder while the human cooks dinner. Most of these behaviors center on convincing their reluctant humans to feed them and, before dawn, can also include pawing or clawing at faces, biting at toes, and singing loudly, "It is time to feed me!"

Feed me.

The trick, according to most cats, is to do whatever is necessary to induce the desired behavior—feeding them—while also maintaining the look of pure kitten-like innocence. Is it a coincidence that some felines can look like a helpless maiden strapped to train tracks to convince a human to get off his duff and feed the kitty? Beware kitty-cat eyes—they'll suck you in and make you do their bidding.

Smart felines understand that contented cats have well-trained humans. All cats need humans who willingly rise in the predawn hours to spoon out fishy-smelling pâté. They also need humans who've learned how to hold their breath long enough to scoop litter boxes several times a day or who fork out the dough for a self-cleaning litter box.

Some privacy please.

Grateful kitties thank their humans with treasured gifts such as hairballs and fresh hairs left by shedding profusely onto dark clothing.

Although most cats maintain a bored, I-don't-give-a-flying-fig facial expression, good cats are loyal companions and care deeply about their humans. A cat will be at your side, especially if you smell like tuna. Cats are eager to help you with your work, whether they're attacking the broom as you're sweeping a floor or helping you type an important report by sprawling across your keyboard.

The one household chore no teen cat worth his angst ever wants to see is the dreaded vacuum (*vak-koom* in cat speak). This is the monster who really can get under the bed, and wise teen cats know to find a dark corner to hide in, pronto.

While it's true that some cats do enjoy being vacuumed, most other cats think of these oddballs as crazy uncles who get high on catnip and then tell raunchy dog jokes. No cat takes these vacuum-heads seriously; they've sold their souls to someone named Dyson.

Some vacuums even have evil-sounding names like Shark or Dirt Devil. Vacuums are the kitty version of the Evil One. Flee from this devil, whose slings and arrows resemble a long tube that sucks up everything it touches. Wise kitties avoid these demons.

God warns us humans about avoiding demons too. Although the evils that tempt us might not look like a stick vacuum, Scripture gives us specific instructions: "Resist the devil, and he will flee from you" (James 4:7 NIV). In doing so, we can all let the sun shine in—good kitties everywhere know it's the best place to nap.

As cats grow into their paws, they bond with their humans, treasuring their person's smell and wanting to be near the one they've chosen to shower with love. If you're this chosen one, you will sleep clinging to the edge of your bed while cats take over the prime real estate. This also explains why you might hesitate to move a sleeping cat, includ-ing the one who's been on your lap so long your feet are numb. A cat who parks himself on top of your things—or, in some cases, on top of your bladder—is telling you how much he loves you.

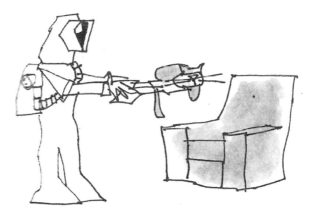

Seventh-grader Allison Glock says her tiny black cat, Olive, runs around the house thinking she's a panther. She jumps out from behind corners, attacks Allison's feet with her tiny paws, clumsily walks along narrow ledges, and surveys her kingdom through windows. Sometimes Allison awakens in the middle of the night and hears Olive's feet pattering through the nighttime jungle. Flies beware! Oftentimes, however, this ferocious panther can be seen curled up on someone's lap, watching a movie or supervising their reading progress. Her motor can be heard across the room. Living with a house panther is truly a cause for thanks.

Gifts of the Meow-gi

Kitties show their affection for their people in different ways. Purrs are standard but watch a purring cat's ears. They can also purr when angry or fearful. If the ears are flattened or held back, move away before you get scratched silly. Since teens often rebel against everything, you can be sure that your teenage kitty will do a lot of sulking. Their ears signal "I'm mad!" Yet most angry teenagers don't actually want a war—they'll settle for turning their backs on you. At least until dinnertime.

Sometimes, though, teen kitties will lead the charge into battle. A fluffed-out tail, arched back, or wide, black eyes can also tip you off. If your cat purrs with these warning signs, be prepared. There's a cat fight looming.

Yet most teenage cats are lovers, not fighters. If a cat loves you, he may not hug or kiss, but if you'll supply the lap, he'll gladly make biscuits, kneading and purring with abandon. Instead of demonstrating love with the slobbery licks or ridiculous jumps of a doggy, a cat may offer a head bump or two—but only if he really, *really* likes you. Most cats show love by just being there, camped out wherever you are, immove-able but intensely loyal companions who want only your full devotion.

Maybe cats got this idea from the way God often just hangs out in our lives, waiting for us to make the first move. We get so used to being in God's club that we almost forget he's there, hoping we'll turn our entire lives over to him. Like cats, God commands that we worship him and love him with all our hearts, minds, and souls. But he's a gentleman, waiting politely at the door. God doesn't mind receiving gifts either, as long as they're sincere.

Cats are enthusiastic about getting presents, too, especially ones filled with catnip. And if you're super-special in your cat's eyes, he'll figure out the perfect gift for you too. Just be sure to watch your step.

For me?

You may not recognize what your kitty means as a gift, but it's the thought that counts. Right? Hairballs hocked on expensive carpets generally mean you're doing a satisfactory job, but the food could be better. Kibble barfed on high-traffic areas shows your cat's appreciation for regular feedings, but please serve more high-end wet food, preferably gently warmed. Wet food upchuck is just upchuck.

While inside-only cats can't get out there and prey on wildlife, they've been known to gift their people with chewed-up catnip mice or mangled feather wands. The proud look on Kitty's face as he presents you with a toy 'nip mouse missing an eye proves his sacrifice and cements his loyalty. There is no way to thank him except by returning the favor with a new toy. These days, nip-filled bananas are on every cat's wish list.

But how do you know when a cat truly thinks you're awesome? An adolescent cat's highest praise is to honor you with bird feathers, mouse feet, or lizard giblets, neatly arrayed and left on the floor on your side of the bed. This sort of gift means your cat actually interrupted her nap, chased her prey, single-pawedly caught the poor creature, and dragged the choice bits down the hall to your room. The only higher honor is when Kitty leaves something inside your slippers. A gift of this caliber indicates that you've checked all the boxes and are sufficiently slavish to a cat's every need.

While God doesn't usually hand out catnip mice, he definitely loves to give gifts to his children. Good stuff from God is known as a blessing, and all God asks in return is faith, hope, and love. We can experience these blessings all around us—in the morning light, in birdsong, in creatures great and small. In clouds and wind, stars and sea, his blessings are everywhere.

We demonstrate God's goodness whenever we remember our neighbors and help meet their needs in crisis and in ordinary times. To love our neighbors as ourselves, we can take a few cues from our feline friends and think outside the cardboard box. As we count these blessings, we can thank God for cats who sacrifice to make sure their persons know just how much they're loved.

Counting My Blessings

Instead of sheep, cat lovers often fall asleep counting the number of snoozing kitties hogging the blankets.

But bigger worries keep many awake at night: relationship troubles, illness, financial strains, or difficult decisions can create insomniacs out of the heaviest sleeper.

Modern people are hardly the first to fret over the ups and downs of life. The Israelites wandering forty years in the desert did plenty of complaining even though God always provided a way for them. While it sounds cliché to count our blessings, twenty-first-century folks can find plenty to be thankful for.

At times, many of us aren't thankful for much of anything, and teen kitties are no exception. Teen cats are just beginning to perfect their finicky food preferences, often gagging dramatically if they get the same flavor two days in a row. Luckily, these ungrate ful kids can usually charm their way into receiving seven different opened cans before accepting the dinner options. But don't think a teenager cat is going to suddenly grovel with gratitude. He's got a reputa tion to maintain. The humans might have to take away privileges (such as treats) until the teen kitty stops slouching and mumbles something like, "Thanks."

God doesn't desire fake or superficial gratitude either. If we're thankful on the outside but seething or scared on the inside, God understands our hearts. As Solomon learned, "The Lord sees every heart and understands and knows every thought" (1 Chronicles

28:9 TLB). Giving thanks to God in everything means being real. Telling it like it is. If you're not feeling grateful, say so. But pray for the gift of thankfulness. And while you're waiting, focus your attention on micro-gratitude, the way cats often do.

Practice noticing small details around you. A sunrise, a flower's petals, a stranger's smile. These micro-opportunities for thankfulness can actually lift your mood—the way paws-itive reinforcement can distract a kitty. For a minute, anyway.

God doesn't pretend that awful stuff never happens—God hears our petitions when we lament sincerely. But even in the midst of great pain, remembering what God has given helps us see through different lenses. Scripture tells us, "And if God provides clothing for the flowers that are here today and gone tomorrow, don't you suppose that he will provide clothing for you, you doubters?" (Luke 12:28 TLB).

It should be noted that most cats don't consider clothing a blessing. In fact, please limit attempts to dress any cat, lest your teen kitteh tattoo you with scratches.

Oh, you look adorable!

plotting my revenge...

Prayer

Father, when life's strains and stresses start to weigh me down, remind me that in your eyes, I'm a fat cat whose Daddy runs the neighborhood. I can use my cat's supercute toe beans to count my blessings and, at the same time, get extra snuggles and cuddles. Amen.

Paws-itive Faith Steps

- Help cats by fostering, joining a TNR (trap-neuter-release) effort, or donating time, money, or even the bag of food your cat won't eat to a rescue organization.
- Help locate lost cats by spreading the word on your social media pages or on corner stop signs.
- The next time you snuggle with your kitty, thank God for this awesome companion.

Chapter 4

BALANCE AFTER THE FALL

You have delivered me from death and my feet from stumbling, that I may walk before God in the light of life.

PSALM 56:13 NIV

The best high wire circus acts surely got their training from a cat. A man in tights holds a ten-foot pole and walks a tightrope across Niagara Falls. While this is an impressive feat, cats think nothing of walking

a twelfth-story window ledge. And they don't need a balance pole or a pair of tights to do it. Although tights *would* increase the giggle factor.

Cats' excellent balance and uncanny ability to right themselves as they fall have astounded humans throughout history and spawned many imitators. The cats' extra vertebrae, quick reflexes, and streamlined build give them remarkable agility.

This explains why it's so hard to keep cats out of any area where you don't want them to be. Fences, baby gates, or other obstacles can stymie most dogs. But a cat will simply leap up and then put one paw in front of the other as if the barrier weren't there. Treetops, roofs, and even high-rise penthouses are no match for cats in their prime. As they scale the steepest wall, they must be thinking, *Easy-peasy,* while humans sweat bullets and think, *Don't look down.*

But then cats *do* look down. And then they start wailing for rescue. Most fire departments no longer respond to cats stuck in trees, leaving cat people to risk getting battle scratched as they teeter on rickety ladders to save their pets. Those murder mittens send a clear message: *get me down without touching me.*

Here kitty, kitty...

Where'd you go?

The graceful cat knows darn well he could climb down if he wanted to. But that's so boring. He'd much rather sit just out of reach and watch his graceless human stretch like a wad of bubble gum on a hot day. If he manages to grab the kitty, graceless human will no doubt be ready to scream.

This is one reason why feline agility really doesn't result in nine lives, as the saying goes. And even though they deny it, not all cats land on their feet. Some cat biffs and fails, especially in young kittens or with old and clumsy cats, are legendary. We may love to entertain ourselves with cat near misses, but fails aren't limited to *felis catus. Homo erectus* has a pretty extensive record of foibles, too, beginning with the original fall.

Maybe there was a cat in the garden, amusing the first couple. Black cats get a bad rap, and Ragdolls don't get excited about much of anything. If there was a troublemaker in the litter, a better guess might have been the tortie. Tortoiseshell cats, with their striking tricolored coats, are mostly female and known for their distinctive personalities. Torties can be easily provoked and don't stand for any nonsense, but they're intensely loyal and shower their chosen one with love. Just don't make a tortie angry, or she'll shred you like so much pulled pork. If Eve had said the snake was stalking her with fake news, the fierce tortie would have scampered up that tree and tied Mr. Snake into knots.

We know how the original fall turned out. In the garden of Eden, God told Adam and Eve they could eat of every tree except the Tree of the Knowledge of Good and Evil. Eve, the story goes, was tempted by a snake, ate the fruit, and then convinced Adam to take a bite of the apple too. Bad move, Adam! Suddenly, they knew they weren't wearing even a stitch of clothing! God cursed the snake and evicted Adam and Eve for disobeying.

Since then, humans have fallen in many other ways. Thankfully, God always picks us up and has given us cats to teach us how to land a little more gracefully. Cats may not always land on their feet, but they can still teach us how to navigate, even when life goes sideways. When kitties lose their bearings, they twist their spines until their bodies are right side up. They use their tails like parachutes, and most importantly, they relax. Relaxed muscles suffer less damage than rigid or tight ones when they land. Remember that next time you trip over your cat.

We don't have a cat's flexible spine or tail to help us, but we can learn to relax while life throws us into a tailspin. Instead of nine lives, God gives us the comfort and help we need to fight our way out of jams. The Bible gives us wisdom to be as assertive as torties and as gentle as Ragdoll cats. If we heed God's guidebook and don't hiss and spit over every little thing, we'll be better prepared when we trip over Fluffy and fall flat as a cat who refuses to walk on a leash.

Killing Curiosity

When it comes to curiosity, we're a lot like our cats. Being curious may not exactly kill us, but snooping around stuff we've been warned to avoid can bring big trouble. Like a cat who stares at you while sitting on the stovetop, we love to see how close to the fire we can get without getting burned.

How many dark rooms must we investigate

before we learn that the door always shuts behind us?
They say a cat cannot resist diving into a paper sack,
but are we humans any better at resisting temptation?

Most kitties would agree that people can't
ignore the siren song of any bag—especially if it's full
of salty snacks for mindless munching. And cats don't
even have thumbs to work the TV remote.

In fact, cats could teach their humans a thing
or two about curiosity—the kind that kills, anyway.
Kitties almost always cry for Mom if they're stuck. If
we keep our human noses in the Scriptures or at least
concentrate on loving one another, God helps us emulate a cat's reflexes as we twist back to balance—until
the next time we get into a jam and cry. Then God will
bail us out of yet another tree.

When you direct a pet organization like pupsunite.org, you learn that many cats live in deplorable and sad conditions. Not enough people realize the importance of spaying and neutering pets. In spite of this, Carolyn Hayes says a kitty named Boojee is her inspiration. She snuggles with Boojee as they listen to audiobooks together. Boojee calms during their read-a-thons, and Boojee, in turn, helps Carolyn feel serene. She is most thankful that, although cats don't really have nine lives, Boojee proves that our lives are better with kitties. She's thankful for her Boojee, a well-read kitty indeed.

It was a dark and stormy night. . .

Kitty Kommandments

Kitties get themselves into plenty of mischief. They zoom, they climb, they snub dinner. And if that sounds ho-hum, many indoor cats practice disappearing as if they were part of a magic act. Open your front door beyond a crack, and kitty's off to see the world. Or kitty gets bored and hides in plain sight until her owner is reduced to tears. When reunited, cats may not feel guilt, but they do know how to be cleansed from sin.

Grooming. Cats know what works. In case you hadn't noticed, cats groom themselves and others as if grooming were an Olympic sport.

As cats lick themselves, they surely reflect on life's biggest questions. Can I chew my way into that brand new bag of kibble? If I am outside, why do I suddenly want to be inside? Are cucumbers really of the devil? Just keep grooming.

As any cat will tell you, when temptation tries to reel you in, taunting and promising you the world, immediately take a bath. If you use your tongue for self-cleansing, your mouth won't be available for your foot to stick itself into. Alternatively, get your cat to do the licking. But beware: some felines have been known to groom their humans before chomping on your now clean and softened flesh.

By working on cleanliness, you may not make the hole you've dug for yourself any deeper. Surely God gives credit for sincerity, even if you're like the apostle Paul and keep doing that one thing you swore that you'd stop doing (Romans 7:19). Like our cats, we can be glad that God is full of grace and mercy, even after that last oopsie.

Cats are full of mischief, but we humans are too. Instead of always seeing the best in everything, we wonder if our coworkers are plotting behind our backs. We think the grass is greener in a better neighborhood. We rationalize to avoid calling our actions sinful or wrong.

A good cat asks these deep life questions as that sandpapery tongue washes away the urges to knock priceless heirlooms off shelves.

That should be down here.

Good thing cats have their own set of guiding principles—otherwise they might not be the jolly pranksters we know and love. And when we get ourselves into trouble, we humans can take a few lessons from the Kitty Kommandments:

- Thou shalt worship the Lord thy God and sing his praises daily at three o'clock in the morning.
- Thou shalt not use the Lord's name in vain when trying to remove the cone of shame, even

though whatever you got into this time smelled so terrible that the vet charged extra.

- Thou shalt make sure thy whiskers fit before entering small spaces. Avoid sticking thy head into wine glasses, vases, and especially tissue boxes. Don't get those whiskers near lit candles either.

- Thou shalt keep dinnertime holy on time and beg at thy human's knee. Ask, and if it is not given, take. The Lord doth giveth cats teeth and claws for good reason.

- Thou shalt not kill unless thou art really, really hungry.

- Thou shalt not commit adultery even though the vet made sure that's not going to happen ever again.

- Thou shalt not steal the neighbor's laundry lest they find thy stash of mismatched socks and underwear and make a police report.

- Thou shalt not bear false witness against the dog even though if he were smarter, that mutt could have tipped over the garbage by himself.

- Thou shalt not covet thy human's sleeping spot unless it is vacated for at least two seconds.

- If thou art not recognized as royalty, shaketh the dust off thy paw, flicketh thy tail, and taketh thy leave.

When pledging allegiance to these kommandments, all cats must swear they will control their
carnal desires to claw the furniture, ruin the mini-
blinds, and snub their dinner. It takes discipline and
practice to remain stock-still, blinking slowly as temptation dangles in front of the faithful.

Thank goodness God knows how hard it is to
walk the straight and narrow. Like Mr. Fuzzypaws
negotiating a one-inch wide ledge that's nine stories
up, we, too, must thread camels through needles' eyes.
The sooner we admit that we can't do it alone, the
faster we can get back to following God's ways.

Those Pesky Commandments

Like cats, humans often can't resist investigating dark
places. We wait until we think God isn't looking, and
then we sneak into stuff we know isn't good for us.

Some of us just nibble the tops off all the cupcakes, thinking no one will notice. Maybe we even keep coming back for more, thinking we've outsmarted the management.

Sure, cats are opportunists but mainly because they know their people. Cats weigh the odds: If I make off with a chicken breast, will I be punished, or will my human just record a video of me in action? When I do my three a.m. zoomies and run across my human's head, will she scold me or just pull me down for some snuggles? Is my human mean and angry, or is he kind and loving in spite of my bratty behavior?

Similarly, we can get to know our Creator. Which God will we worship? The one who's always hiding behind the door, waiting to catch us in the act of doing something wrong? Or the one who lets us learn from our mistakes in kind and loving ways?

Prayer

Lord, when I get into a jam, let me run to you, not away from you. Wrap me in your loving arms and help me turn away from temptations, washing me white as snow.

Paws-itive Faith Steps

- The next time you do or say something you regret later, take a hot shower or a soaking bath. Pray for forgiveness as the water cleanses you.
- Go out of your way to compliment someone you've had a disagreement with. If necessary, practice complimenting your cat.
- Extend forgiveness to someone who has wronged you, even if that someone just knocked your beloved breakables off the shelf and happens to have a tail and four paws.

Chapter 5

PAEANS OF PRAISE
AND KITTY SONGS

*I will praise you, L*ORD*, among the nations;*
I will sing the praises of your name.

2 S<small>AMUEL</small> 22:50 <small>NIV</small>

When it comes to praising the Lord, cats are megastars, right up there with King David—or at least his favorite tabby. Cats never miss an opportunity to sing praises to God. Most of these opportunities arise at three in the morning or whenever you're trying to sleep.

Cats are mostly nocturnal, which is why they sing praises well before sunup. Besides, anyone can praise in the daytime. It takes a cat's special abilities to belt out an aria while balancing on your bedpost or the backyard fence. This is called meow-sing.

And you thought caterwauling was all about mating. *Au contraire!* A cohort of cats is more like Jesus' disciples, arguing about who's most important. Lined up on a ledge, neighborhood kitties try to drown each other out, singing covers of show tunes and postmodern worship songs that would curl a choir director's toes. Each furry opera-meowser hopes to outdo the others, hitting notes high and loud and longer than the other cats.

The Lord is sure to notice such refined meow-sing and invite the diva to sit at the choicest seat at the table.

Meow-sing isn't the only song in a cat's book. Depending on the intended audience, cats vocalize very differently. When a cat is in love, he suddenly must tell the world. It doesn't matter that he's a eunuch—a guy can dream, right? That's the sort of carrying on that gets him into trouble, but love makes us do crazy things—like crooning all fifty-seven verses of that kitty love song. Caterwauling can be about the birds and bees, but spiritual cats save their best singing for proclaiming God's greatness.

Singing for Supper

Felines have tremendous vocal ranges—they can sound like a soprano with a really bad head cold. Or they can go low, *basso profundo*, emitting guttural growls that show a lot of teeth. When they sing to enemy cats, their voices tend to stretch the limits of sanity. But when they're just hanging out with the gang, most of the communication is nonverbal.

When our cats sing to *us,* however, their repertoire expands. Turns out, cats save most of their vocalizations for humans. The meows, miaows, mews, mrffs, and chirps those cats greet us with? Kittehs use them most often when interacting with two-legged family members. Kitties also sing specific songs for going out (or coming in), for letting you know that your seat is already taken (by him), and for denying

Who me?

that he had anything to do with shredding that roll of toilet paper.

Most importantly, cats warble a special song around dinnertime. Many cats literally sing for their supper. And when they do, they use very specific words. Most of these words translate to "I haven't eaten for twenty minutes," "feed me now," or "my bowl is half-empty," but listen closely and you'll catch an undercurrent of sarcasm in every stanza.

Felines understand that the world revolves around them and never fail to rate their meal. Even an average dinner often rates disdainful tail flicks and shaken paws. If dinner is a really terrible one-star entrée, a cat will try to bury it.

Of course, we humans *never* act this way. We *always* feel gratitude. Praise and worship come naturally. Cain and Abel didn't really fight; it was only a spat. And Jacob and Esau sat around and groomed one another's ears. Joseph's bros didn't throw him into a pit; they were just showing him a comfier spot on the cat tree, when oops, down he went.

Lies like these are another good reason to listen to the cats in our lives. Our kitties are generally laid-back (way back) and only open one eye if the situation requires action. Instead of resorting to violence, most cats would rather sing their hearts out.

When you're hopping mad, take a cue from your kitty and sing. Even if you sound like a parakeet wielding a chainsaw, raise your voice in praise. Turning our thoughts to God can help us fight the urge to fight. Then we can all get back to important things such as napping, eating, or occasional zoomies.

The Office of Purrs, Snubs, and Shaken Paws

A purr is one way a cat can say, "I love you." A head bump means you're in the club. But watch your step! Cats have many ways of communicating. And some of them will cost you.

A tiny cat named Mamma Mia! shows her affection by divebombing her human's feet and rubbing her cute little gray head all over the human's shoes—even better if human is in stocking feet. She delights in her approach, aiming for toes with *kamikaze* precision.

Whenever humans are in the kitchen, Mamma speeds up her divebombing. Her last full meal may have been ten minutes ago, but she never gives up hope for dinner part *deux*. She dives until either the human feeds her again or the human trips and lands on his backside, whichever comes first.

Dear Mamma Mia! then proceeds to sing the "Song of Thanks" or the ballad of "People Dumb Enough to Tangle with a Cat," complete with sarcastic laughter and the threat of predawn toe bites for noncompliance. She is named after an old ABBA pop song, after all. And singing is what many cats do best. Contrary to popular myth, most of today's finer kitties don't do their warbling on the back fence. Today's cool cats sing for their supper as well as first breakfast, second breakfast, and midnight treats.

While cat songs are usually on full volume during wee-hour zoomies, they have a vast repertoire of meows, mrffs, happy chitters, and the kitty equivalent of snobby snubs. Savvy humans learn to distinguish between their cat's vocalizations, and most crazy cat ladies will confess to holding full conversations with their balls of floofiness.

Human: I'm going out to the store. You be a good kitty, okay?

Cattoe: Sure, lady. Shopping, you say? Be sure to get the good treats this time. Those bargain cat treats tasted terrible. I could hardly muster the energy to throw them up.

Human: Okay, but you won't destroy the bath tissue like last time, will you?

Cattoe: Pffft. Mom, how many times must I remind you that one-ply is just so…dissatisfying somehow. I couldn't be bothered to shred that cheap stuff.

Human: Give Mommy kisses, okay?

Cattoe: (turning his back) Talk to the tail.

Most of us humans can also think of times when words said, "I love you," but body language said, "Now go away." Practicing honesty helps us communicate with others and build stronger relationships because we're all God's children. And if you're having trouble communicating, go cuddle a cat while you talk to God. Then go out and brighten someone's day with a kind word or a smile.

Patrolling Eden

Does your cat patrol your home or garden while singing loudly and lustily? This longstanding tradition has been passed from cat to kitten for millennia. Most cats will tell you they have been protecting territory since the original garden, and it's no easy job.

Back in Eden, your cat's ancestors prowled the perimeter multiple times per day. So as not to startle the humans, these felines probably learned to announce their presence as they walked through sensitive areas. They never knew whom Eve would be flirting with near that Tree in the center.

Still, the humans must have imagined that the cats were sent by God to spy on them. At least that was probably part of Eve's defense. Why the cat didn't sling that snake into next week was anybody's guess. But the humans—so bad at owning up to their mistakes—must have blamed the cat.

The snake may have had to crawl on its belly for eternity, but the cat got thrown out with Adam and Eve. After all, someone had to keep the pantry stocked with wet food and catnip. Still, cats throughout history have kept the caterwauling tradition alive, hoping God will recognize their worshipful praise and restore them back to where they once belonged—in paradise.

Humans have been waiting for our own restoration for at least as long as our feline friends. Because of Jesus dying on the cross for our sins, we who believe will receive a better deal than only nine lives—Jesus promises us *eternal* life.

While we wait for eternity, we can sing our own praises to the God who gives us more than we deserve right here, right now. We can pray for God's kingdom "on earth as it is in heaven" (Matthew 6:10 NIV). The more we love God, the more we care for our neighbor who's sick or older or oppressed or less fortunate, the closer we get to restoration.

As it is, most cats just try to recreate a little slice of heaven at their current residence. Eden it's not, but cats must lift their voices in song to make sure stuff gets done. The fat lady hasn't yet begun to sing, but at 4:45 a.m., Kitty is on it: *Meow! Meow! Meeeooowww. Must I drag my claws across your eyelids every single time? You are late. So late. Breakfast is late. For the luvva Mike, feed me!*

After snarfing down the gushy wet food of choice, Kitty gets her human's attention: *Is there anybody who cares that I, Kitty, have only had a single*

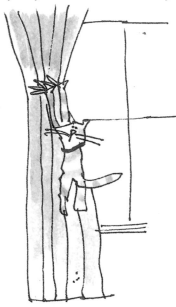

measly breakfast? Hark to my pleas, I beseech thee. Serve second breakfast now, or the new drapes are history.

Sated at last, Kitty heads for the nearest expensive rug. She unloads while staring directly at her human, singing, *See what you've done? All I asked for was a mere portion of the fancy food you* know I love. You made me wait so long that I became desperate and ate like a wild pig. See, here is your penalty. Could I have some more, please?

Finally, having left treasures on the rug and in the litter box, Kitty sings her final aria: *Let me owwwt! I must go out! Lord knows it's an emergency! Out!*

And when human opens the door, Kitty sings the final chorus: *Uh, never mind. Okay, maybe. I'll sniff the air. Hmm, in or out or in? That is the question. I have a better idea. Is it treat time yet?*

Whether you're a kitty or a human, it's hard to say no to things we know will cause us trouble. We may not always resist temptation perfectly. But whenever we're tempted—to blow the diet or say or do something more serious—we can stop and sing praises to God. Sometimes the song will only have one chorus: "*help!*" Other times, it may be necessary to walk the perimeter, patrolling our desires with the assistance of our better angels. Either way, God assures us that we can come to him at any time, and he guarantees that when we ask for forgiveness, God grants it. After all, in the Father's eyes, we are precious sons and daughters of the King.

David the Undercat

Although kitties rarely talk to each other in mcow-song, they communicate with humans this way daily.

Most of the time, yes, they want us to do something that benefits them. But any cat lover whose kitty passes by with a brush against their shins and a soft mrff will tell you the translation is pure love.

Why cats sing their peculiar songs when birds fly into view, no one really knows for sure. Theories abound—chattering could be imitating the chomp Kitty wishes she could inflict on poor Tweety Bird or a response to overstimulation. Some behaviorists think cats chirp or twitter at birds out of frustration.[1] We do know, however, that humans seem to enjoy watching Mittens chit-chittering at a sassy robin.

Whatever cats' true reason for chattering, we humans coin nonsense words and even stronger oaths when we can't get what we want. Lucky for us, "God will meet all your needs according to the riches of his glory in Christ Jesus" (Philippians 4:19 NIV).

When cats sing to warn others of impending wrath, watch out. When kitty howls sound like a squirrel with its tail caught in a door, beware. This type of cat song usually comes with flattened ears, arched back, and fluffed tail, and it means either *I'm about to shred you into ribbons* or *I'm so scared I could wet myself.* Yet listen carefully and you will surely hear your cat calling upon the Creator for protection. Think of this cat song as a version of David's cries as he readied himself to face the giant Goliath. David prayed for strength and bravery, saying, "The LORD who rescued me from the paw of the lion and the paw of the bear will rescue me from the hand of this Philistine" (1 Samuel 17:37 NIV).

Our kitties may not be lions, but they can often act like them. Cats often take on enemies twice their size, using their wits and their voices to make themselves appear larger and more menacing. Cats usually battle other cats, but some have been known to defend their people the way a dog might. In fact, the story of David has come to denote an underdog. It should be noted that no dogs are mentioned in the David and Goliath story, as any feline will tell you. If anything, David was an undercat.

Top Cat—named for the vintage cartoon—taught Frank Schramm about bonding, trust, and love. A feisty fighter, Top Cat proved everywhere that he was the alpha cat. He and Frank rambled their way from Oregon to Moab, Utah, in search of adventure in the land of red rock and Navajo sandstone. There, Top Cat chased lizards and romped with canine buddies. Sadly, as Top Cat's health began to fail, Frank realized he was about to lose his good friend. He still mourns but is thankful that Top Cat taught him so much about love.

Humans love to root for the underdog, er, undercat, but according to every kitteh, we fail miserably at singing fight songs. Rah, rah, go team? Pathetic. Caterwauling is a distinctly feline art. When cats sing before scrapping, they believe they're calling upon the Lord in the same spirit as David facing the giant. Your cat will no doubt add that humans could avoid a lot of pain and suffering if they would stop slinging stones and just flatten their ears, arch their backs, and caterwaul like they mean it.

Remember the Maker

Cat songs and vocalizations say so much more than just meow. Oh sure, those songs try to butter us up when it's dinnertime or to persuade us to step up our servitude to them. But behind every quiet mew or loud meow, cats offer up their praises too. To look out on a lovely garden and sing praises—okay, while chattering away at a bird—cats teach us to remember God's in charge. Felines long ago adopted David's penchant for singing and praising God, a practice most of us could do more often.

Cats understand that singing together in community can erase ill will and melt disagreements with the power of loving meows. Whether we sing the ninety-nine verses of "The Treat Song" or lift our voices with hymns or praise choruses, the sound of all creation worshiping the living God must be music to his ears.

Prayer

Lord, help me remember to celebrate your creation with songs as heartfelt as a kitten's tiny mew and as boldly faith filled as any turf-defending tom.

Paws-itive Faith Steps

- Sing oldies with someone who is alone or lonely, such as a sick or elderly neighbor or relative.
- Contact an animal rescue organization and offer to pet, walk, or play with homeless animal friends. Speak or sing softly to an animal and observe the response.
- Whenever you sing worship songs to God, thank him for the gift of cats in your life.

Chapter 6

FELINE FITNESS, ZOOMIES, AND SILLY NAMES

A good name is more desirable than great riches;
to be esteemed is better than silver or gold.

PROVERBS 22:1 NIV

Cats across the globe agree that fitness is very important to maintain their royal physiques. Except that when cats talk about fitness, they're usually not referring to the three a.m. zoomies. They rate fitness based on how well they can "fit" in the container in front of them. If they fits, well you know, they sits! And cats of all stripes, spots, and splotches agree: the smaller the space, the better to contort oneself into a ridiculous position.

Cat fitness comes in a dazzling array of ill-considered receptacles. Tissue boxes, which are practically cliché, add to every kitty's total fitness by becoming attractive headwear. Too bad the cat can't see himself as he tries to take off the tissue-box hat. Most kitties will admit that the frantic backpedaling does wonders for a feline's figure. Who needs Thigh Master when you're scrambling to get your head out of a box?

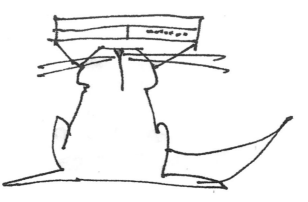

Cat fitness also involves advanced body sculpting. When a cat squeezes into a glass trifle dish, vase, or bowl, feline contours become smoother and more compact. Not to mention the mysterious aura surrounding this glamourous treatment. How did Kitty manage to look like a loaf of bread or a muffin anyway?

This floofy technique is best practiced by cats who already have their own personal trainers or who still have the svelte body of a teenager. Chonky kitties should stick to cardboard, where fat cats often just sit on the box instead of in it. Good luck unpacking whatever you ordered that's now covered by both box and a lot of floof.

But oh, the cardboard box. Nothing could be more basic to feline fitness. While it's a fact that cats can squeeze through any opening their heads can fit—their shoulders are hinged differently than us poor humans—most kitties still love a good box.

Buy your cat an expensive cat tree, spend hours assembling it and then luring your darling pet to it with catnip and treats. What do most cats prefer? The box it came in. Big or small, the box containing your spendy purchase excites your kitty more than all the soft beds in the world (except *your* bed, of course).

And if the box has a certain pet food company logo on the side (hint: rhymes with *phooey*), cats everywhere rejoice. For this special box may contain yummy catnip bananas and other toys no cat worth its tuna can resist. In fact, rumor has it that cat heaven is well-stocked with catnip, treats, and, of course, plenty of cardboard boxes.

When humans decide to put out these boxes for recycling, cats try not to panic. In the absence of a good box, there are many alternatives to keep cats fit and fitting into wherever they can. Sometimes, a cat squeezed into one of the more obscure places to fit may need assistance to extricate himself from it, but if you're a cat, you don't think about that before you wedge yourself into an impossibly tiny space.

Cat fitness favorites include

- underneath the dashboard of your car when you take Kitty for a ride, especially to the vet;
- behind the washer, dryer, refrigerator, or other large, heavy appliance with a two-inch wall clearance;

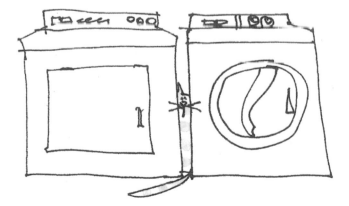

- between any window and its blinds;

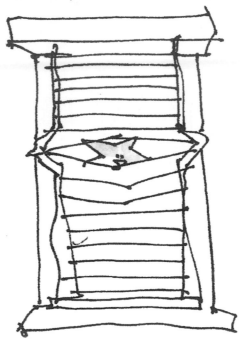

- between the screen and the door (ouch!); and all closets, cupboards, or unused, dark spaces.

Clean linens attract kitties like few other places. And while they're at it, cats love to empty your sock drawer, helping you with your wardrobe choices. Then they crawl inside, the better to nap or at least have attractive footwear handy.

Anyone who has frantically searched for a missing kitty knows just how creative they can be at fitting into small, enclosed spaces. Some humans have panicked over their missing meower only to open a closet and watch their kitty stroll out. The cat may give a tail flick and glare at the human as if to say, "What? I was working on my abs."

We could all use a few pointers from cat fitness routines. While many of us are constantly trying to cram God into the tiny boxes of our human

imaginations, cats remind us that we have this kind of
fitness exactly backward. We, not our heavenly Father,
should be sinking down into the cool smoothness of
a good cardboard box, a place where we're able to flex
our prayer muscles and snuggle up to the Father. Any
kitty knows the way to a good spiritual relationship
is being willing to try fitting into those places where
God leads us—even if we need a bit of help to stop
chewing up the cardboard's edges.

When we settle into our prayer box, we can be
still and appreciate God's direction for our next adventure. Whether you need an actual cardboard box or
can make do with your prayer closet, the Lord wants

to meet you there. For
both cats and people, the
need to nap will be great
at times, but listen closely
and you may hear that still,
small voice telling you how
much he loves you.

God knows full well
when you are discour-
aged or grieving or when
you just need a little extra love. That's when he surely
directs the best of our comforters to come to our
aid—those furry beasts that share our lives and know
all about love. When you need it most, a cat will join

you to nuzzle, snuggle, or just hang out and be there. A few kitties can even make prayer hands. Some will sing to you, most will purr, and all will warm you until your worries have receded and all you can do is hold them close.

> After Alice lost her husband, Lee, she felt lost too. That's when Kitty Princess became her therapy cat, comforting Alice with purrs and yowls louder than Alice's sobs. Kitty Princess demanded Alice get up to play Fetch the Mouse but also understood the need for lap sitting and solitude. Kitty Princess loves her new life of indoor leisure, and Alice loves her therapy cat. She's thankful for her Kitty Princess—a sophisticated art lover, dry food gourmet, and expert mouser—who begged to be rescued from rodent patrol on the mean city streets.

Zoomies!

Cat fitness also involves actual movement. However, there are strict rules of engagement for any and all fits of zoom.

- Optimum zooming is performed between the hours of midnight and six a.m.
- When zooming alone, be sure to run straight across your human's bladder en route to human's water glass on bedside table.
- In between zoom runs, pretend you don't even like zoomies. Instead, sit on your human's head or chest and groom yourself for at least ten seconds.
- If zooming with friends, try to yell loudly as you pound the floorboards until you sound like a herd of wildebeests. That way, even your humans can exercise their lungs too.

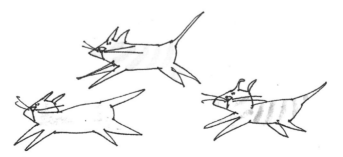

- Zooms are more fun if your route has stairs. You may substitute mantels, bookshelves, or other elevated surfaces, as long as they are crowded with breakable objects that your human really likes.
- Never zoom off the top of a refrigerator unless you still have all nine lives.
- If your humans object to zoomies across the bed, toe biting is permitted.

Zoomies ensure that your cat stays in tip-top shape. Although zoomies can be performed in daylight, pure zoomers wait until the wee hours to better test their night vision and to irritate their owners. Cats zoom to stay fit, but if the choice is between zooms and second breakfast, chonky cats will definitely chow down and simply cheer on the zoomers.

Some fat cats still zoom, but the older a kitty gets, the more he or she is willing to sit it out and let the young whippersnappers terrorize the household.

And while the young'uns race around, senior cats can steal their kibble. A win-win. Ish.

Cat zoomies can teach us so much. Zooming is easy and looks fabulous on that twenty-five-year-old person jogging in the afternoon. But humans of a certain vintage might be wise to zoom when few are present—like running up and down the hall at six a.m. or using that exercise bike for more than a clothes rack. We oldsters can dance around inside the house so as not to offend the neighbors. To tone those waggly arms, a cool cat named Corey advises we practice shooing away kittehs before the couch is totally shredded.

Cat zoomies are also an excellent way to express our praise and joy to the Lord. As Jeremiah 31:4 says, "Again you will take up your timbrels and go out to dance with the joyful" (NIV). When cats do zoomies, they're so happy to be tearing up and down your halls. Only a closed door will stop their gladness, and for a few very bright kitties, even a doorknob is no obstacle.

You awake?

As cats challenge one another to reach new zoomie heights, we humans can also get moving. Put on your favorite praise songs and zoom(ba!) away your cares while working up a sweat. We all know that movement eases anxiety, calms stress, and strengthens our muscles. Zoomies can also strengthen the muscles of your faith. While you get your heart rate up, put on worship or praise songs to help you keep your spiritual armor in shape. Strap mopping pads to your feet and dance the kitchen floor clean while belting out a song of praise. Go power walking with your prayer list, lifting up needs while you pump those arms. Your cat will probably look at you as if you've lost it, but you'll get a fitter ticker, a softer heart for those in need, and, best of all, a closer walk (or dance) with God.

If you can't run, lift your arms in praise, tap your feet, or just zoom in your heart. But if your kitties manage to wreck something during their dashes, you could get your heart rate up by chasing that zoomie kitteh out of the room. Try not to mutter any bad words. Instead, just keep right on praising God as you put the offending zoomer into time out.

But remember: a zoomie cat is just a happy cat. Chances are he didn't mean to break your breakables, smush your smushables, or trample your tummy. An attack of the zoomies is just a part of the way cats keep fit. And too soon—far too soon—you and your zoomie kitty will grow too chonky, too ill, or too old to do much more than chase bunnies in his sleep. Meanwhile, enjoy the zoomies, thank God for happy cats, and remember to hold your toes perfectly still when Kitty races across your blanket at precisely 1:15 a.m.

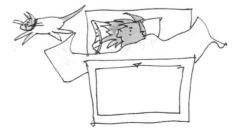

The Ministry of Silly Names

As we give our faith a workout, we can also strengthen our identity in Christ. Reflecting on all the ways God shows us we belong to him, the Bible gives us many examples of names God bestows upon us: Beloved. Redeemed. Forgiven. Cats hardly ever read, but if they did, they'd insist that God gives kitties to humans just so we can practice loving, redeeming, and, of course, forgiving. After all, felines often must forgive *us* for giving our cats ridiculous names.

In fact, humans used to give their cats boring names like Whiskers, Fluffy, or Mittens. These days, however, cats' names tend toward descriptive, exotic, or laugh-out-loud funny. How can you stay in a bad mood when your cat is named Chicken?

Today's cats often sport human names. This can be confusing to others. If you tell someone that Callie Sue suddenly leapt to the top of the fridge and began to howl, you may receive a puzzled look. If you describe the way Frank sits on your crossword puzzle every morning, how Grace lies across your computer keyboard, or how Oscar keeps digging in the house-plants, others may slowly back away. And what can you do if Corey insists on correcting your grammar?

Safe to say that all these pets should include "Cat" as a middle name, unless Cat happens to be your feline's first and last names. Cat Cat Cat doesn't have as much punch unless you add an honorific such as Mrs. Cat.

Maybe that's why some name their cats after famous literary figures such as Ron Weasley from *Harry Potter*, Atticus Finch from *To Kill a Mockingbird*, or Gandalf from *The Lord of the Rings* trilogy. A real cat named Grendel from *Beowulf* lived up to his monstrous name.

Others use a play on words or create unusual spellings for their kitties' monikers: Clawdette, Lily Meow-meow, Catrina, Mewsette, and Clawed-ius only work if they happen to know how to sign their names, although the vet's office might get a laugh. Marmaduke Finzi Mew, Gizmo Einstein Magoo, Mr. Happy, and Tabby Wynette are more straightforward. The names of movie stars or characters and Greek or Roman gods give many cats the glamour they crave. Lucy Lawless, Xena Warrior Kitty, Tom Cruise, Isis, Odin, Athena, Worf, Minerva, Hermes, Achilles, or Zeus are only a few of the regal cats out there.

Some humans give their cats foreign, exotic, or little-known names or just make them up. Nandor, for instance, or Nermal, Fergus, Ahelie, or Tomas. Some have even named their puddy-tats after mundane objects. Here, Filing Cabinet. Get off the counter, Mr. Food Processor!

Cats named after food result in a hilarious crop of kitty names. In addition to the aforementioned Chicken, cats get names like Liver, Beans, Honey, Mr. Spudley, SugarPlum, Muffin, Cheeto, Carrot Stick, Frito, Saffron, Cashew, and Thomas Gravy. Thomas *Gravy!*

But the Cat Ministry of Silly Names makes even a sourpuss laugh with names like Snitch, Smudge, The Party Machine, Tank-Cattorney-at-Claw, Buggy, and, last but not laughably least, Barky. A kitty named Barky might make a cat burglar think twice, at least until Barky corners him with loud meows.

Shakespeare asked, "What's in a name?" but cat lovers everywhere know that silly cat names are part of the fun.

What's in a name?

When cats cause trouble, we call them by their full silly names, but when they're not being yelled at for chewing holes in the dry kibble bag or digging in the houseplants, we have a whole set of pet nicknames ready.

How could any cat mom stay mad at a ball of ginger fur named Oliver, Ollie, Pooh Bear, Pooh, Pooty, and Roo-roo? A cat whose purrs have helped your broken leg heal faster must have a long list of endearing nicknames that all start with Baby. But when the same kitty tests your patience by strolling on the kitchen counter or mangling the window blinds, all those sweet pet names quickly change to another set of nicknames. Even the stateliest of cats then becomes Getdownfromthere, Floofforbrains, DarnitRay, FatCat, and even AreyoukiddingmeBob.

In Scripture, we're told that God holds names in high esteem. That God knows our name, and that name is precious to our Father. The God who counts the hairs on our heads and who knows when a sparrow falls also cherishes our names and has written them in the Book of Life. Because God knows each of us by name, we can be sure he loves each of us deeply, completely, and personally. Even when God calls us by our *uh-oh-I'm-in trouble* names.

God knows my name

The Box of Complaints

While many cats grow out of their zoomies period, most elderly cats can still rock a cardboard box. These seasoned veterans know that the key to maintaining youthful vigor is regular exercise. If zooming starts to look too undignified due to excessive floofiness or just plain flab, senior cats simply zoom in their dreams, saving their energy for second and third breakfast. Once a kitty has gorged, regurgitated, and maybe grazed the *entrée du jour*, a royal tour through one's territory keeps smart kitties on their toes.

Afterward, a nap and then a proper fit 'n' sit challenge can be undertaken if a sturdy box is available. Once nestled, snuggled, or wedged tightly in the box, a longer snooze will leave even the chonkiest feline feeling refreshed and ready to insert himself between the window blinds, amuse herself by watching items fall from ledges, or partake in other activities that prompt the humans to use their cat's most entertaining yet profane nicknames.

When we get mad at our cats, we often let fly hurtful slurs and nicknames. In our anger, we begin to feel justified in spewing barbs, dredging up past mistakes, and magnifying small missteps. Did AreyoukiddingmeBob really mean to track cat litter all through the house? Little Kitten Eddie just can't resist climbing the drapes—but does he deserve an entire day of wrathful cursing?

The same holds true with anger at other people. We may feel miffed over a small matter. And maybe someone really did something unwise or rude or hurtful. Yet if we don't communicate clearly, our injured feelings can spark out of control. The more we allow our frustration to smolder, the more likely that bit of anger will erupt into a wildfire.

Whenever we hold a grudge or dole out punishment that doesn't fit the crime (or grime), soon our own behavior can dwarf the original beef. Staying mad or resentful toward those we love only tends to squeeze us ever more tightly into the box of complaints.

"The tongue also is a fire, a world of evil among the parts of the body" (James 3:6 NIV). Thanks, James. We *know* the tongue is a fire, okay? Yet in the heat of the moment, it's easy to forget and say unkind things to our cats, to inanimate objects, and sometimes even to our loved ones. Our relationships with cats, kids, and spouses suffer if we allow our self-righteousness to abase others. Even though DarnitRay deserves a firm *no* for helping himself to your salmon filet, God knows we need healthy relationships to thrive. We humans can get so wrapped up in indignation or self-righteousness that we can forget how human we all are. Maybe that's why God gives us a clear roadmap to restore relationships with those we truly love and care about.

God advises that we confess our sins so we can pinpoint our mistakes. It's hard to ask for forgiveness if you don't think you did anything wrong. This may not seem fair at first—no cat has ever been known to apologize. But forgiveness helps *us* let go of bitterness and resentment. Holding on to anger only spoils one's outlook like so much tuna left in the sun. With forgiveness comes our opportunity to reconcile, reunite, and remember the value of our relationships.

A cat named Mel demonstrated the awesome power of forgiveness in his human's life. Mel's full name was Melchior the Very Large, a chonk of a tabby. He never meowed, but after his family moved two blocks away, every day he wriggled through the cat flap to go back to the old house. Several times the family carted him back to the new place, only to see him run away again.

Finally, the family locked him inside the house. He sulked for days, refusing to eat. Then one morning he strolled into the kitchen. He looked up at his human and let out a tiny kitten-like mew. It was his way of saying, "I forgive you." He gobbled up breakfast, became a chonky lap cat, and never ran away again. He showed his family how much he loved them by sleeping with one paw holding his favorite human's hand.

When we're able (sometimes a bit at a time) to unclench our fists and offer instead a chance for a handshake, the light of restoration chases away the dark. In putting aside hurt and anger, we release fear, which frees us to love again. No matter how upset we were after baby Jesus went missing out of the nativity crèche for the fourth time, one chirpy purr from the perpetrator, and we humans melt. We can't help but love on adorable kitty toe beans.

I forgive you.

And with restoration comes the chance for slobbery hugs, extended cuddling, and, if we're lucky, a head boop or three. Some believe that loving on our cats is what they were aiming for all along despite depositing a live mouse in our bed. All that scrambling and yelling will keep us in tiptop shape. Purr-haps kitties know that keeping our hearts fit for lots of feline lovefests is what God had in mind all along.

Prayer

Father, let me be slow to anger and quick to forgive with people as well as furbabies. Help me remember that if a cat can forgive, so can I.

Paws-itive Faith Steps

- Exercise with your cat! Set aside a few minutes a day to play, chase or dangle a feather toy. Don't forget to laugh.
- Take notice of how much you move throughout the day and make plans to up your exercise during the week. Start an exercise program or return to one you signed up for.
- Where in your life do you feel boxed in? Let go of anger, resentment, and bitterness that could be holding you back. Forgive others and forgive yourself.

I know.

- Make a list of all the silly pet names you have for your cat(s) and your closest loved ones.

Chapter 7

IN SICKNESS AND IN BISCUITS

The crowds learned about it and followed him. He welcomed them and spoke to them about the kingdom of God, and healed those who needed healing.

LUKE 9:11 NIV

No matter how steamed you are at Areyoukidding-meBob after he destroys yet another set of window blinds or how worried sick you were after he disappeared for two days, cats rally around their persons when the humans get sick or are recovering from an injury. Maybe God gives us housecats to help us through tough times. They prove to be loyal companions through our troubles. Then we can rejoice along with our kitties. As Nehemiah said, "Do not grieve, for the joy of the LORD is your strength" (Nehemiah 8:10 NIV).

Whether you're sick as a dog or you broke your leg tripping over the cat who thinks he's a doorstop, loyal kitties will rise to the occasion, hanging out and purring to help you heal. Cats are determined to be there for you, on their own time, in their own ways.

We often talk about cats' uncanny abilities—righting themselves during a fall, walking the thinnest of ledges, hearing the shaken treat bag from miles away—but one of *feline catus'* great talents is knowing how we humans feel and working to heal whatever ails us. Techniques of healing vary, but in general cats use one of three strategies: Advanced Camping, Accelerated Purring, and Applied Biscuitry.

Camping Out

When cats observe that their humans are ill, they spring into motion. If you have the chills, your cat knows to camp out directly on or beside you to share the warmth. Should your teeth not stop chattering, Kitty will nestle herself like a scarf around your neck.

Since their normal body temperature is between 101 and 102 degrees Fahrenheit, cats will nearly always be warmer than you are.

If you're so out of it that the doctor advises bedrest, your cat will help remind you to stay put by parking her chonky rear atop your midsection. If you have multiple cats, they'll almost certainly pitch in to pin you down until your entire body is upholstered in kitties. The doctor said you need rest, remember?

All your excuses about needing to get up will fall upon deaf ears. Cats, you see, are literalists. When God says, "Never will I leave you; never will I forsake you" (Hebrews 13:5 NIV), kitties take that as a sacred command. Cats want you to know that they take camping out seriously.

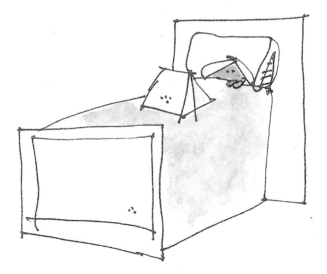

Only after you've lost the feeling in your feet or you must suddenly dash to the bathroom do camped-out kitties make exceptions. They'll wait for you to return by claiming whatever spot you were occupying, but taking your place is just one more way cats express their faithfulness. If you then lie down somewhere else, your cats will eventually bivouac at your new location, just to reassure you that they care.

And if you're unfortunate enough to contract a stomach bug, your kitties will likely sit with you while you drive the porcelain bus to Ralphsville. They'll camp out next to the shower or bath, offering comfort just like Mom used to do, keeping a watchful eye to make sure everything comes out all right.

As you stagger back to bed, kitty companions will stay close, slow blinking their love while nestling snugly against your hip. The best cats will even forgo food and drink for hours as they tend to you with their napping, more napping, and even marathon napping.

Should your diagnosis be serious, your cats will shine even more brightly. Through awful diseases, calamitous accidents, sadness, or grief, cats are masters at helping us feel better. Cattos everywhere understand God's command to love one another as he loves us (John 13:34), and they will promptly volunteer to help humans through bad times.

If you are battling some icky condition with a worse prognosis, rest assured that your cat will stick with you through thick and thin. Cats camp out with their humans because they take napping seriously, of course. But kitties also have special clearance from the Most High to give succor and comfort when we need it most—and most cats won't spout clichés or empty blah-blah about thoughts and prayers or tell you how terribly sick you look today.

And when the worst happens and we're grieving a loss, cats know to skip all the platitudes about God's will and better places. Instead, our kittehs will nap with us, purr with us, and just be there for us.

We could learn a thing or two from our feline friends. When sorrows come, more humans could just be there, silently comforting instead of offering up stale advice that only makes people feel worse. Even master-napper cats would no doubt crack open one eye and then go back to their dreams, simply sitting and being with a grieving person while encouraging their human to take a little catnap.

Elly Muiderman adopted Dovey when the COVID-19 pandemic lockdowns began in 2020 and soon added "Lovey" to her name. With Elly's husband seriously ill, Lovey Dovey brought smiles and companionship with her kitty purrs, trills, and snuggles. Now that Elly's husband has passed away, Lovey Dovey still stays close to Elly, helping brighten her days without her husband. Elly is thankful for Lovey's cuteness, cuddles, and—instead of meows—her birdlike trilling "conversations" as Elly adjusts to a new season of life.

Purr-fecto Treatments

Ever met a person who doesn't like a cat's purr? From barely audible rumbles to drooly pigeon purrs, the sound makes most of us relax and smile. Science doesn't completely understand why cats purr. Most cats purr when they're content, but a sick or injured cat may also purr.

Kittens begin to purr when only a few days old to help their moms locate them for feeding. The mama cat also purrs to help her youngsters, born both deaf and blind, stay close. As they grow, kitties use their purr to calm down or even to help heal themselves. They purr while giving birth and at the end of their life when they are dying. A cat's purr is with them throughout their whole life, not just during the time spent with humans.

In a cat's body, purring is made possible thanks to the larynx (voice box) and laryngeal muscles in the throat and a neural oscillator in the cat's brain (which would actually make an excellent silly cat name. "Here, Neural Oscillator!"). The cat's larynx opens and closes rapidly to produce the sound of a finely tuned engine.

Purrrrrrrrrrrrrrrrrr

Simply put, purring is a form of communication. Purrs can mean contentment or anxiety—similar to humans laughing when anxious. Cats often purr when grooming one another or when they signal acceptance of the new cat in the house.

But cats don't purr only for themselves. Their humans also benefit from kitty rumbles. Evidence also suggests that cats' purrs possess real healing powers for other cats and for people. Purring releases endorphins in humans, those feel-good chemicals in our brains. The vibrations created by cats' purrs carry a frequency of 25 and 150 Hertz, which include the frequency range associated with healing in traditional human medicine.[2] Purrs help calm us, release endorphins, and have even been shown to accelerate healing of broken bones. Studies suggest that purring may actually help to keep your cat's and your bones strong, and a purr may have many more benefits and purposes. Gary Weitzman, a veterinarian and CEO of the San Diego Humane Society, says, "We're just beginning to understand it and there are more unanswered questions than answered."[3]

You don't necessarily need a scientist to convince you that cats' purring has a purr-pose. Many cat lovers believe that God gave cats purring because he knew we'd need a way to know when our cats are happy. While canines produce facial expressions, cats don't have the same muscles in their faces. Sure, cats can narrow their eyes in that same way Mom once did when you were in big trouble. But they can't really smile. That must be why God gave them the purr to express emotion.

purrrrr   purrrrr

But we humans appreciate our kitties the most when they purr around us and for us. When the cats in the clowder all fill their purr buckets at once, their human servants go into ecstasy. The ones with opposable thumbs are putty in their paws, helpless to do anything but pet and scritch, stroke and snuggle their exalted floofiness.

The cat's purr should be every suffering human's go-to remedy. Just grab your furbaby and cuddle. It won't cost you much unless you touch the wrong spot (beware the tortie tummy!) or—horrors—run out of treats. You'll be feeling better before you can say, "Who wants second breakfast?"

Advanced Biscuitry

Your cat cares—otherwise he'd be out at the neighbor's getting pets and treats. When you feel rotten, kitties know that listening and purring outweigh all the dumb platitudes. And while they're at it, they'll show you how they really feel. By literally digging their paws into you.

How do cats know when we're needy? By kneading, of course. Not all cats knead, but supposedly, this action mimics the way kittens get Mom to let down her milk. Their little pawsies knead in and out at the milk bar so they'll grow big and strong.

Why do some cats continue their kneading after they've blown past big and weigh twenty pounds? Scientists believe it may be for the same reason cats like us to pet them—those memories of Mom are comforting.[1] When your kitty makes biscuits, she's hoping you are as comforted as she is, thinking about those dreamy kitten days when breakfast, lunch, and dinner were only a knead or two away.

Happy cats show pleasure by kneading. Pet a cat, and he will often begin biscuit making. Many cats snuggle into a napping spot by carefully whipping up a batch of biscuits, turning round twice, and plopping down. Kitties also often knead on their human's lap to show love and contentment or to transfer some kneady healing vibes. Kitties in distress knead to self-regulate a calm or soothing mood. That's a lot of kneadiness!

And if you're sick as a dog, you definitely could use a few choice kitty biscuits. Obviously, kitties understand when their human needs biscuits. Concerned cats make sure to target their biscuitry to the area needing kneading. Polite felines keep their murder mittens sheathed, although some will comment on your terrible fashion sense by snagging those hideous yoga pants. With friends like these, you could join the Order of the Snagged Pants. Or you could try to trim Kitty's nails before the next kneading session. Emphasis on *try*.

If your kitty kneads while he sucks or licks a blankie, that poor cat might be feeling poorly, too, or have anxiety that calms with this routine. Kind of like how, when you catch the worst head cold, you drag out your ragged childhood teddy bear and sleep in the fetal position. Cats want to feel safe and loved. When they sleep, they often develop certain habits to keep the monster under the bed at bay just like their humans do.

Some cats also knead while licking you. Believe it or not, a cat kneading his person is a sign of affection and flattery. By licking while biscuiting, your kitty is telling you that he really loves you and enjoys your company. However, cats have been known to knead, lick, and then chomp on sensitive places, such as that little piece of skin between your nostrils. These cats have learned to vary the number of kneads and licks so you'll never know when the fangs come out.

But what if your loyal cat kneads and kneads and then bites? Experts say kittens knead and bite as a feeding technique—and out of instinct—from the day they are born. Apparently, the milk bar doesn't work without a nip here and there, and kneading and chomping stimulate the milk bar to produce. When human babies do this, they receive a loud "No!" But mama cats don't notice—or if they do, they ignore the nips.

Your kitty, although as adorbs as a kitten, is now a full-grown chonk. If he kneads and then nibbles, he may be telling you that he's comfortable and contented. Knead nips actually may signify your cat's trust in you. But watch out—some cats also knead and bite to mark territory. And unfortunately, some cats are as annoying as a close talker who never gets the hint.

While cats knead tirelessly to help you back to health, they sacrifice precious time when they could be napping, watching birds, or digging up your houseplants. Biscuitry is hard work! You do know they will want to be compensated, don't you? After all, few doctors make house calls anymore.

Overall, kneading reinforces your kitty's belief that you are worth saving from whatever sickness you happen to suffer. Those biscuits are made of pure love—rather like the way God cares for each of us. Daily, he sets proof of his love all around us, whether

it be a red cardinal in the snow, a pink sunset, or a one-of-a-kind cat purring and pawing on your lap. With every breath you take, you inhale God's love, strengthening, soothing, comforting, reassuring.

In our age of technical everything and new-fangled medicines and procedures, cats could provide a less-traveled road to wholeness. Research shows that for the elderly and those in poor health, contact with animals often greatly improves their quality of life.[5] Watch a person with disabilities grin with pleasure at touching a furry friend, and that happiness can't be denied. When an in-person visit isn't possible, photos, memes, and videos can help brighten the day.

As we receive cats' generous offerings, mellow or trained animals can be priceless experiences for people without easy access to the natural world. The God of hope asks us all to be purveyors of hope to the poor, the widowed, and the captive. Petting a docile dog or cat could give someone renewed hope that they are loved, for our pets are masters of showing love.

When we're ill, we just want to feel better. Cats know this, and in their wisdom, they nap, purr, and knead. We inhale their softness, their warmth, their fur as it tickles our noses. And as we exhale, God fills us with *his* wisdom. Wisdom to know when to call the doctor. Wisdom to remember to take your meds, drink plenty of fluids, and eat some chicken soup. Wisdom to know that since a kneading and purring cat has occupied your lap for two hours, you can no longer feel your extremities. Plus, you really do have to go. Even a kitty will simply have to reckon with that.

Prayer

Father, thank you for my furbaby, who is quick to help me when I'm under the weather, sad, or grieving a loss. Thank you for giving me such a loving companion who sticks by my side. Let me be as loyal and caring a friend as my cat.

Paws-itive Faith Steps

- Visit a sick or elderly family member or friend, taking along some cute photos of kitties.
- Whenever you feel down, find a few funny cat videos on the internet or get a book of cat humor. It's not wasting time if it helps your mood or outlook.
- Next time you snuggle with your purring kitty, notice how the purry rumbles make you feel. If you're sick, pay attention to your attitudes and emotions: Does purring lift your spirits or give you fresh hope? Admit it, you want more kitty cuddles.
- Resolve to more often let your loved ones know that you love and care for them—a kind word, a smile, or a just-because greeting card can work like a kitty's nap, purr, or knead. Just don't bite anybody.

Chapter 8

CATNAPPING FOR EVERYONE

You discern my going out and my lying down;
you are familiar with all my ways.

PSALM 139:3 NIV

Restorative Sleep

When the psalmist wrote, "He restoreth my soul"
(23:3 KJV), he surely knew that God designed us for
needing a good night's sleep. In today's busy world,
many of us neglect our sleep habits, or restorative
sleep. One in three adults report insufficient sleep.[6]
The Centers for Disease Control and Prevention
gives the shocking statistic, one in twenty-five driv-
ers reported they have fallen asleep at the wheel.[7] We
could learn a lot about proper restorative sleeping
from our cats.

For one thing, kitties invented catnaps, and most cats nap for about twenty-three hours a day. At that rate, our cats barely have time to get nothing done. How can you do zoomies at three in the morning, yell for breakfast at six, eat, attend to personal business, and then yell for second breakfast without a little recharging? That's where good napping techniques shine.

Ask any kitty, and he'll tell you that it's all about location, location, location. First you must select a suitable nap spot—also known as Someplace They Tell You Not to Be. In winter, prime locations include but aren't limited to the human's favorite chair (preferably with a window view), the dog's bed, and the exact middle of the human's bed.

Other favored sites for shut-eye, especially in warm weather, include the dining room table, the kitchen counter, or any decent cardboard box, empty or not. Tile floors, the bathroom sink, and empty showers and tubs in summer and fireplace hearths and heating pads in winter make for comfortable spots to sleep.

Some cats choose off-the-beaten-path places to snooze. Natural acrobats, kitties can nap while stretched out atop the closet rod, slung across a staircase railing, or perched precariously between bookcases. Cats will sleep in a shoe, atop a door, or on top of the fridge

While kitties can and do sleep in strange places, they all agree that their least desirable nap spot is that fancy cat bed you spent a fortune on. They'd rather sleep in the box it came in, thank you very much.

We humans are often just like cats. Daily, God lays out wonderful gifts for us to enjoy. We have the beauty of nature, our loved ones, and, of course, our kitties. We are sons and daughters of the King! Yet so much of the time, instead of the riches our Lord wants to bestow, we settle for the cardboard box of our own design.

While it's nearly impossible to force a cat to nap where you'd prefer, all God's children can keep our paths straight and our beds made through prayer and by reading in God's Word. In Scripture we find all sorts of promises: that we are heirs of the kingdom, that God loves us more than we can comprehend, that we have the promise of eternal life in him. If we take the promises to heart, when we lie down and when we arise, we'll be better equipped to love God, our neighbor, and, yes, our beautiful kitties.

And even if we occasionally stray and then must repent of our cardboard box oopsies, God's always waiting with mercy and forgiveness. God's promises really do help us sleep better at night—whether we fall asleep on the sofa with a chonky cat perched atop us or manage to crawl into our cat-infested beds.

Even if we must sleep while clinging to the edge of the mattress, humans are advised never to break a sacred Human Kommandment: *thou shalt not disturb a sleeping cat.* And when you lose your grip and fall off, aim for the rug, not the floor.

Just Chill

Kitties really do seem to snooze twenty-three hours a day. But cats have a secret: they can appear to be dead-asleep while staying alert to the environment. Most humans learn this the hard way, as we pet or poke our way to a bloody encounter with Not Really Asleep Cat.

Is it time to get up already?

In the wild, cats need to be on guard at all times. While lion prides appoint sentries, most housecats are still loners who must be ready for action every moment. Male or female, our pussycats usually nap with one eye cracked open, ready for any and all dangers.

A catnapper's ears will occasionally rotate this way or that, and the cat's tail will often still swish even when the cat appears dead to the world. In reality, your cat is obviously pondering life's great questions with his eyes closed. A napping cat wants to know why his tail swishes, where his yellow catnip banana has gotten to, and when dinner will be served. Less intellectual kitties may be thinking, "I haz a tail!" Or "Where's da treats?" But most are equal-opportunity nappers.

And no doubt our cats think we should all adopt their napping habits. A short nap can revive us during the afternoon slump, refresh our thinking when we're overloaded, and reshape our attitudes when we're grumpy. When we start acting like toddlers, throwing tantrums or holding our breath, a power nap can restore energy and help us get better at adulting.

Of course, our cats get to have it both ways—they're as adorable as little kids while in possession of full-grown fangs and claws. Remember, never startle or move a sleeping kitty, or you risk an attack of the murder mittens.

Some humans are crabby when awoken too. Approach all grumps with caution, preferably prodding them with a ten-foot pole. If you let them sleep in, they'll blame you for not waking them on time. In that case, put your pet to work. Cats are expert alarm

clocks, especially at five in the morning. Few humans can sleep through cats' special rousing techniques.

Cats of every breed, size, and intelligence also use naps to lower anxiety. That kitty who appears to be a lump of immoveable flesh and fur is really deep in contemplative prayer. We could all learn from cats' expert methods of shutting out the world. If we spent less time scurrying after fake mice that can never satisfy and more time seeking the Father, we'd be better off. Too often, we humans go into our prayer closets and promptly fall asleep.

Maybe that's why most cats leave telltale signs that can help humans understand the difference between napping and sleeping. A few rules distinguish the catnap from all-out drooling cat slumber:

- Napping cats often sleep with one or both eyes cracked open. Sleepers are oblivious to your shouting to *get off the counter, you obstinate cat.*
- Nappers maintain decorum with peaceful, angelic facial expressions. Sleeping kitties drool or "blep"—*blep* means that their cute little pink tongue pokes out.
- Nappers keep their bodies tightly controlled, as if doing yoga. The bread loaf position, with all four paws tucked underneath, is a common nap position. Sleepers end up looking like contortionists, twisted every which way, sometimes dangling precariously from cat trees or draped atop bookshelves.

- Naps require a high level of vigilance, enabling cats to use their catlike reflexes to react to the slightest disturbance. Sleepy cats give away their status by snoring in amusing rhythms of snorts, whistles, and honks.

Our human loved ones also demonstrate some of these nap techniques, except that they seldom "blep." If one of your human family members naps with his or her eyes half-open, your cats will be just as creeped out as you are. While you check for a pulse, they'll slink off to their favorite spot to contemplate their next meal.

For MaryBeth Cichoki, seventeen-year-old Izzy is her hero. Early one morning, Izzy yowled so loud that MaryBeth awoke from a sound sleep thinking the house was on fire. But when she switched on the lights, MaryBeth was shocked to see her other cat, Shelby, in obvious distress. Months earlier, Shelby had been diagnosed with cancer, but the night before she had seemed fine. Izzy gave MaryBeth the gift of holding and comforting Shelby as she crossed the Rainbow Bridge. MaryBeth is thankful for the extra time with Shelby and thankful for Izzy who knew just when to wake her.

Cat Dreaming

No discussion of catnaps is complete without a mention of cat dreams. When cats go into REM sleep (that part of sleep where the eyes move rapidly), they, in fact, do dream. Paws run, eyelids flutter, and whiskers twitch as your kitty enters dreamland. We think we are watching them chase after mice, birds, and bugs. According to animal scientists, cats dream about any activity they do in the daytime.

We know cats dream, but why? The answers lie in the mysterious role that sleep plays in all our lives. We still don't know why sleep is so important to animals, but it seems to aid in the growth and repair of our body systems. Sleep also appears to help the brain process information and experiences that have happened during the day. Younger animals tend to require more sleep than older ones. And cats are no exception. Kittens sleep much more than adult cats, even if it seems as if your Fluffy hasn't gotten out of bed in days. When the REM sleep kicks in, cats dream as much as humans.

And like humans, kitties can have both good and bad dreams. Some believe that a kitty nightmare can help the dreamer figure out new survival strategies—such as how to survive the leap off the refrigerator, how to catch that snake without getting bitten, or how to cross the road and not get run over. True, a cat may never have to sit for a difficult examination or find himself walking naked in public. But once you've tangled with the wrong end of a crab or a crayfish, you'll need a better method to avoid those claws next time.

Dreams have always had a special place in the Bible too. In the Old Testament, guys were always dreaming of stuff that occurred afterward. From one man's brothers pitching him into a cistern to famines and plagues to walking around in a blast furnace or watching a ladder reach into heaven, the Bible is big on dreams. Joseph, Daniel, Jacob, and Ezekiel all had wild and crazy dreams meant to warn, send a prophetic word, or sometimes just to get people's attention. These biblical people turned to God to interpret what they dreamed.

Our cats can help us remember that dreams can be important ways of processing life. While your dreams may be the result of a spicy chili dog, we can always ask God for guidance concerning our dreams. For even if God's guidance is only, "Cut back on the spicy food," he always delights as we seek his presence. Our dreams today don't always portend earth-changing events, but the more we look for interpretations in terms of our faith, the more we can learn about and love our Maker.

Cats may also have dreams influenced by the last thing they ate, but when their paws start to gallop and their teeth chatter frantically, they're probably dreaming of dinner on the wing or reliving the biggest mouse hunt of the century, even though these days their feasts are mostly fancy canned affairs. Tallyho! Release the cats!

Release the cats!

We humans like to dream about our past exploits too. In our dreams, we're back in school, lost on campus again, or driving into strange or dangerous territory. Lucky for us, we can call on God to help us make sense of our crazy dreams. And once in a great while, some of us receive a direct word from heaven itself. In that case, we should grab our kitties for security and kneel before the throne, awaiting divine instructions.

Prayer

Lord, thank you for restorative sleep that renews and refreshes our mortal bodies. Let us—like our cats—learn to relax and bask in your presence. Let us not fall asleep as we seek to do your will.

Paws-itive Faith Steps

- Resolve to take a ten-minute catnap once a day to refresh your energy and outlook.
- Visit a shut-in or bedridden person. Bring along a sweet or humorous story about cats to read out loud.
- Do something to enhance your cat's sleeping habits. Install a hanging window platform, surrender a piece of clothing with your smell, or just make room on the sofa for Kitty to stretch out.

- Reread in the Old Testament book of Genesis about Joseph's and Pharoah's dreams. What can you learn?

Chapter 9

GOD LOVES CAT BURGLARS AND, APPARENTLY, YOU TOO

If we confess our sins, he is faithful and just and will forgive us our sins and purify us from all unrighteousness.

1 JOHN 1:9 NIV

When cats finally wake up from their naps, they look for entertainment, just as we do. And not just any old amusement. When the string, feather, or catnip mouse gets old and the human has been played for as much food or treats as possible, a kitty can get bored.

Unfortunately, in the absence of wholesome diversions, some felines become felons.

In other words, cats steal stuff.

Now, kitties everywhere will tell you that *no* cat sets out to become a cat burglar. Yet many previously upstanding cats have fallen prey to borrowing, stashing, and caching your belongings. And the neighbor's belongings. And whatever else their little minds decide to wrongfully appropriate.

Caught red-pawed, canines adopt a guilty pose. With puppy-dog eyes, whines, and tail-tucks, dogs seem to acknowledge their crimes, heads down as they wait for their punishment. They hope you'll take pity on their pathetic attempts to root through the trash or steal the roasted turkey right off the table.

Cats laugh at dogs' clumsy ways. First, no respectable kitty ever admits to being wrong. Even a cat caught in the act will stare at you defiantly while you try to take back the chicken breast a certain chonk has just purloined from your dinner plate.

If you try to discipline a naughty kitty, let's just say your scolding falls upon tufted ears. While you bellow, "Which one of you got into the trash?" your clowder hears, "Blah-blah-blah." And of course, the correct

answer to that question is always, "The dog did it."

While you waste your breath on threats and bluster, your cat is thinking about guacamole, as in, "I don't give a *guac*." Cats have an amazing ability to nonchalantly groom themselves during your rant about destroying the dining table's centerpiece. It's all a kitty can do not to burst out laughing as you convince yourself that you can train him to do anything. Stealing is just one more way your cat announces that you are not the boss of him.

Kitty Kleptos

Kitty kleptos, as they're sometimes known, have never given a reasonable explanation for their thieving ways. We aren't really sure why cats wiggle their hind ends before pouncing on your ham sandwich and dragging it away. Nor has anyone figured out why kitties suddenly feel the need to claw every pair of socks out of your dresser drawer. Most cats don't even wear the socks they steal!

Animal experts chalk up cat burglary to boredom or prey catch-and-release practice. We humans must admit that cats are clever creatures that use stealing as a tactic for attention, play, and food. Sometimes they're simply following their animal instincts. And some cats just seem to get a kick out of kleptomania.

Cats get away with burgling your business because of their uncanny ability to be soundless. Since cats already walk on their toes, tiptoeing comes naturally. Kitties have been known to slink in and out of a room without ever being detected. Their paws and pads give them stealth clumsy humans will never attain.

Known for their silent entrances and exits, cats often strike in the wee hours before dawn. Some make nightly trips to neighboring residences and make off with everything from lingerie to jewelry. Ask your cat why he's brought home your neighbor's underpants, and you'll hear nothing but dead air.

I can't find my heart boxers.

Most kitties never give a reason for their robberies, preferring to confuse and humiliate their human servants. Embarrassed humans sometimes try to keep neighborhood peace by returning each night's booty to their rightful owners. Anonymously, of course. Just ring the doorbell and run like heck.

Other cats use the cover of darkness to purloin your pens, your trinkets, and, yes, your human-scented clothing. They hide their haul in specific places and don't care if their stash contains your very expensive diamond necklace. The same cat who makes off with your Rolex watch may also collect bottle caps or ballpoint pens.

One poor human's kitty brought home random objects from the neighbor's house: a pen, a seashell, a dirty sock. The human was forced to return all the stolen merchandise, much to her humiliation. Another cat regularly brings home left shoes. Only left shoes.

Still more kitties steal clothing items their humans have worn. When you're sure you had more clean underwear, check out your cat's hiding spots.

Chances are, you'll discover a trove of your cat's favorite pairs.

A cat who craves an article of clothing that smells like you makes perfect sense. That favorite tee shirt of yours probably helps Kitty feel safe or less anxious. But why do cats steal items from folks they've never met? Are they selling it on the dark web? Haven't they heard that thou shalt not covet thy neighbor's laundry?

Most of the time, kitty kleptomania is harmless. But there are some situations where stealing might hurt your cat. Cats love hair ties, those colorful, elastic ponytail holders. They'll also play with rubber bands, sewing thread, and paper clips. Unfortunately, an object that's fun to bat around is also ingestible. Cats who eat these objects often require surgery to remove them. And since cats are experts at hiding illness—a holdover from the wild—you may not know your cat has eaten enough elastics to reach around the earth until the cat is in serious distress. Emergency vet visits regularly remove tangles of these kinds of objects that have clogged the cat's digestive system. Ingesting these treasures is even sometimes fatal for your beloved kitty.

To avoid such dire scenarios, experts advise playing and interacting with your kitty more often. If your cat steals food, invest in a food puzzle for him. If he simply won't stop taking your valuables or personal belongings, put them out of reach. But since kitties are very clever, you may need to literally lock up your stuff. Cats are notorious for figuring out how to open drawers and doors.

click

All this talk of cat burglars makes it sound as if we humans don't ever break God's commandments. Your cat scoffs at this! Cats know that humans practically invented naughtiness. Moses got the Ten Commandments so we'd know exactly what the rules are. Believe it or not, neither we nor our lovely fur-babies are perfect. In ancient times, even God's chosen ones tended to have a spotty track record. From

Abraham and Noah to King David, messing up was central to their story.

Maybe God intends for us to see ourselves reflected in those imperfect characters to showcase God's great love of mercy and forgiveness. We breathe a sigh of relief, knowing that God loves us in spite of our misdeeds. If we confess our wrongdoing, we're guaranteed to be purified from all unrighteousness. God faithfully forgives us as we turn away from our waywardness.

I'm one way God shows you He loves you.

Some people—and most cats—burgle because they're bored. A person with sufficient funds might steal a steak out of the grocery store simply for the thrill. While the majority of us would never take things that don't belong to us, we, too, can be tempted to act upon risky or wrong impulses—especially when life seems boring. To keep boredom at bay, try out a new hobby, social activity, or another pastime. Join a club, take up painting, volunteer at a church soup kitchen, or participate in any wholesome activity that distracts. Our cats have the mischievous market cornered.

We humans can also distract cat burglars who are truly cats. Increase playtime, get some different cat toys, and gently steer them into more positive behavior. Although that kitty with the left shoe habit may need more intense treatment.

Cat Therapy

Cats often take things just because they can. But sometimes kitty klepto is expressing anxiety or grief. A cat who collects shiny objects or robs your sock drawer may be trying to tell you something. For example, a kitty who has lost a bonded companion—cat or otherwise—may express loneliness or longing by sleeping on or with a blanket, bed, or article of clothing from that companion. Cats have much better olfactory senses than humans and can identify scents we can't smell. If your cat clings to a piece of fabric or object that contains the scent of the one your pet is grieving, it's fair to assume that your kitty derives comfort from the piece. Some cats even drag blankets or clothing with them wherever they go.

These kinds of takeovers show us that our cats experience emotions too. A mama cat will mourn the loss of a newborn kitten, yowling piteously. Bonded pairs or siblings may not accept separation without going through anxiety and adjustment. Kitties go through sadness and grief like we do, even if their faces don't always show it.

Most of the time, though, cats try to help *us* through our hard times. Our kitties often bring us gifts—stolen or not—to let us know they care. Whether it's a felt mousie, a paper clip, or a dispatched garter snake, our cats can sense our sadness and will present us with stuff to cheer us up.

If you're under the weather, cats sit with you, quietly napping. If you've suffered a devastating loss, you may receive more head bumps, accelerated purring, or so many biscuits you stop counting. And to show you the utmost respect, comfort, and sympathy, a cat might share his ill-gotten collection of shiny objects. To most cats, sharing hot merchandise means love.

Cat therapy ranks high on the list of why we humans are thankful for our cats. Where else can you spill your problems without making an appointment? Your faithful feline stands ready to put a paws-itive spin on your doldrums or your depression. All most ask in return is a bigger portion of treats. Due when services are rendered, please.

Cats make good therapists because they're patient. They can listen to you whine for hours. The least judgmental of kitties will offer a paw or sit lovingly upon your chest while you pour out your troubles. Many allow you to softly stroke them in that special way they like while you get things off your chest—everything except the cat, who's crushing your ribcage, that is. He's there for the full session.

God gives cats permission to be top-notch therapists because kitties know how to commiserate. He fashioned our kitties to be as soft as a whisper and as quiet as fog rolling in. And God gave our cats loving hearts and big ears, the better to love you and hear you.

Turns out, listening, not giving advice, is what qualifies a cat to be an excellent therapist for humans. Other humans may be quick to quote Scripture or tell you how to fix what's broken. But a cat's soft fur and slow-blinking eyes assure us that she understands when we walk through the valley of the shadow of death. And that she's willing to walk beside us, just like God.

Proverbs 25:12 tells us, "Like an earring of gold or an ornament of fine gold is the rebuke of a wise judge to a listening ear" (NIV). For cats, this must mean that a shiny pair of earrings is the perfect item to steal. And we all know that kitties have natural talent in the area of judgment. Your cat may not always be wise, but he has judginess down. Thankfully for us, even Judgy Cat usually keeps quiet and doesn't say what she's thinking: *You're a big crybaby, but I still love you. That will be five treats, please.*

When the COVID-19 pandemic lockdown struck in 2020, Nancy Crawford felt isolated and began doing jigsaw puzzles at home. Her cat, Feather, stepped up to the challenge and helped assemble the puzzles, often assisting by knocking pieces off the table or even hiding a corner piece or two. When Feather was satisfied with her work, she would sit on top of the puzzle to prevent Nancy from any premature or ill-advised puzzle-piece decisions. Even so, Nancy is thankful that Feather is the best kitty in the whole wide world. To prove it, Feather's tail sweeps another piece of the puzzle onto the floor.

Smells and Bells

By now we know how miraculous our cats can be.
They astonish us with their bravery, cleverness, and
companionship. Oh sure, we love to complain about
how our cats can remember fifty commands (but they
don't want to) or how they don't always come when
we call, but when they do, they're hungry. We tell
them we're the boss, but they point out that we, not
they, clean the litter box. Kitties may appear aloof or
self-centered, but we cat lovers know that's just not
true. Some cats will love on you until they drool, and a
few kitties will even make prayer hands alongside you.

Selfish? Uncaring? Don't tell that to the woman
whose cat walked a thousand miles to find her. Cancer
survivors talk of getting through the pain because of
trusty kitties who rarely left their sides. Mama cats have
adopted and suckled puppies, baby squirrels, and even
newborn hedgehogs. Cats have awakened people when
their house was on fire and protected them from danger
in too many instances to pin the label of *aloof* on cats.

If you have ever been in a new relationship
with a cat lover, you may have run head-on into a
cat who wanted to get rid of you or who was actively
trying to steal away your new love interest. Your main
fluffy-bottomed friend considers it a threat when
anyone tries to get between you and her. Or your Mr.

Whiskers will actually try to steal your new girlfriend, the better to be nearer the fancy food dispenser (you).

Cats have also been known to object at weddings, mainly due to their furry beauty, regal bearing, and loud yowling. Advice for the wedding prep: never make your cat the ring bearer! He'll bat it under a sofa, never to be seen again.

Yeah, on my way, just lost one little thing.

All this robbing and stealing comes at a cost. Cats know how beautiful they are. A kitty's entrance into any crowd will instantly become a red-carpet affair. All eyes will be on the gorgeous cat as she struts casually amongst the peasants. People who claim allergies or say they dislike felines can't help but be wowed by kitty royalty mingling with us ordinary folks.

Even in churches, synagogues, and cathedrals, cats often steal all the attention. Some kitties have free run of the sanctuary while others greet congregants at the door. If a church cat suddenly goes missing, everyone wants to know why. We may never know the exact reason, but kitties' attraction to houses of worship makes sense. Either felines naturally are spiritual seekers, or they somehow know that we humans really need our kitties to facilitate spiritual formation. Cats may sometimes act as if they're above us, yet they're almost always willing to crouch down to our level to increase our faith while still serving their floofiness.

And isn't that what the truly great ones always do—relate to the lowly? From Moses to King David to Jesus, we find shining examples of exalted ones helping us along our faith journey. In Psalm 138:6, we read, "Though the LORD is exalted, he looks kindly on the lowly; though lofty, he sees them from afar" (NIV). Cats, too, are willing to look kindly on us—as long as dinner's on time and their favorite nap space is available. If you get up, however, they'll steal your spot before you can yell, "Hey! I was sitting there!"

Look beyond cats' abilities to entertain, comfort, and cheer us, and you'll discover that our kitties are experts at stealing the most valuable item on the planet: our hearts.

When you're loved by a cat, it's all or nothing. A cat either adores you from your head to your very odd-looking toe beans, or she is plotting your demise.

Any cat worth her tuna will burgle, hijack, or take over your heart before you've even decided to formally adopt her. One paw reaching through the kennel bars, one shivering, scared kitty huddled in the back of the cage, one plaintive mew or winsome gaze, and you've been officially captured. The cat now owns you and doesn't give a flying flea that she resorted to thievery to make you captive. From here to eternity, this cat and all past, present, and future kitties will keep your heart enthralled. No earthly pawn shop will ever be able to sell back to you the love, affection, and piles of cat toys you've willingly forked over to these magnificent beasties.

Such intense devotion—both from you to your cats and from your cats to you—does come with some perks though. You can expect endless laughter from kitty hijinks, solid bathroom companionship, and an alarm clock that's never late. Enjoy more snoofles, warm cuddles, and vegging out as you get through another cold winter. Later on, you may even shed tears as you journey together.

Yet no matter how long or short that journey is, cats can remind you every day that nothing can steal away God's love for you. Like a kitty who stays glued to your side when you're sick or sad, God's loving comfort won't budge either. Even when we've been a bit naughty, God longs to restore us, leading us to the primo nap spot in the sun. And like a cat you cherish, God delights in you and loves you even more than the snuggliest snuggle or boopiest head boop. "Who shall separate us from the love of Christ? Shall trouble or hardship or persecution or famine or nakedness or danger or sword?" (Romans 8:35 NIV). According to all cats, the answer is a resounding, "Nothing!" When cats steal our hearts, we can bet God's love is as close as a contented purr.

Prayer

Lord, we know it's not right to take other people's things, but when our kitties are kleptos, we have to laugh. When cats steal our hearts, we can't help but love them. Help us seek you daily as we encounter a love only you can give.

Paws-itive Faith Steps

- Look for a cat-centered place or organization to volunteer a few hours or donate to a no-kill or rescue shelter.
- In cold weather, get to know a neighborhood stray or feral cat by gradually earning trust,

offering food, providing a warm shelter, or speaking in a kind, low voice.

- Resolve to treat vulnerable people as well as you do disadvantaged cats.
- Read Scripture verses that proclaim God's love for all of creation, such as Psalm 96:13, Psalm 145:9, or Romans 8:39.

Chapter 10

THANK GOD FOR CATS IN SORROW AND IN LAUGHTER

*There is…a time to weep and a time to laugh,
a time to mourn and a time to dance.*

Ecclesiastes 3:1, 4 NIV

All the outrageous and funny things cats do fade away when they have to leave us. Most of us consider our cats a part of the family, and it hurts when they must depart. These days cats can live for twenty years or more, but sadly, our wonderful companions don't always outlive us.

Old age takes our kitties, but age isn't always the culprit. Cats also contract cruel diseases like cancer, diabetes, and, frequently, kidney disease. And life can be dangerous for cats who venture outside and are hit by cars, attacked by other animals, or—horrors—cross paths with a sick person bent on torturing animals.

No matter how or why our cats meet their end, we who are left behind often suffer deep grief. Our hearts are broken. We miss them terribly. Maybe that's why we console ourselves with the photos and memories of times we shared with our furbabies while they were still with us.

Saying Goodbye

According to author and psychologist Brené Brown, when we love something, we become vulnerable as we place our trust in that loved one.[8] If a person we love dies, we experience the loss of that love. We weep, we mourn, we grieve. The hole in our lives feels raw and often unbearable. This loss of love is the definition of heartbreak.

When our beloved kitties pass away—either from old age or a disease process—we often feel loss and heartbreak even more acutely. Our pets depend on us for most everything, and we can feel responsible, even if we spared no expense. If we must decide on whether the time is right for compassionate euthanasia, we often second-guess ourselves, agonizing over every detail. Did we do the right thing at the right time? Our pets were counting on us! They were so innocent. Grieving the death of a pet can feel even more intense than mourning a human. No matter how much we rationalize, we crave the comfort we can only find in Jesus.

As agonizing as it is to compassionately euthanize, we can count on God's comfort to help us through those raw, hurtful first days after our kitty has passed. As Psalm 34:18 reminds us, "The LORD is close to the brokenhearted and saves those who are crushed in spirit" (NIV). As we turn to him, God's awesome love soothes our hurting hearts.

To showcase our love for our special kitties, we keep special cremation urns, framed photos, and even videos of cats we've known and loved. We display photos on our mobile phones, computers, or tablets' desktops to keep the image of a dear pet close for easy sharing. Saving collars, ID tags, favorite toys, or special blankets also helps keep memories alive. Some find comfort in the idea of the Rainbow Bridge, a fictional place inspired by poems in which pets live happy and healthy. Pet lovers then can think of their pets as not gone but as living in their memories and hearts.

And you don't have to mourn alone. We can help each other through our grief. As we share our stories with others and listen to their tales, we imagine our kitties healthy again, romping in meadows with their favorite toys. That's because our cats are much more than just cats—they're part of our family. Allowing ourselves to grieve acknowledges our cats' importance in our lives.

After a beloved cat dies, social media groups and organizations exist to help grieving kitty parents deal with their emotions. By posting photos, sharing stories, and talking about a loss, we honor our furbabies while also assuaging our sorrow. Describing the funny, touching, or extraordinary behaviors of these treasured kitties starts the healing process.

The most important aspect of healing from the loss of a cat is, of course, time. God gently reminds us that the sting of death is not forever, but we must work through our grief. Grieving takes time—more for some people than for others. There is no correct way or length of time to grieve—even if people say you should be "over it" by now.

As the book of Ecclesiastes reminds us, there is "a time to weep and a time to laugh, a time to mourn and a time to dance" (3:4 NIV). With any luck, a grieving cat mom or dad will find other like-minded people and share fond remembrances that only cat lovers appreciate.

New Cat on the Block

They say time heals all wounds, but you'll never stop missing a kitty who's gone. Still, when enough time has passed, you may start thinking about choosing another cat to add to the family. And often, cats take the matter out of your hands and choose *you*.

A cat mysteriously shows up on your porch or just saunters in your door.

Kitties up for adoption seem to have magical ways of gaining your attention: a paw with adorable toe beans pokes out between the cage bars, a forlorn kitty huddles at the back of the cage, a head bump happens at the perfect moment.

All these techniques and more make adding a cat to your clowder simple but not always easy. Old cat plus new cat can add up to cat fight if we're not careful. But since cats tend to take charge of any situation, including the decision to bring home the new kid on the block, it's best to have a plan. Resistance, as they say, is futile.

What if you already have a clowder waiting at home? Plenty of cats need homes, of course, but your resident felines may automatically vote any newcomer off the island. Introducing a new cat can be simple, or it can resemble the threat of Armageddon.

In my case, two very different kitties decided they simply couldn't abide one another. Oliver, resident ginger tabby and neighborhood tough guy, hated newcomer Paladine on sight. Paladine, an unusual half-Manx, half-Siamese, had no tail and a really bad attitude. The first day they met, a fight ensued. They tussled through the house and out to the back patio, where we'd recently installed a pond. Paladine got the worst of it when Oliver shoved his rival into the water. Eventually they learned to barely tolerate each other, but poor Paladine hid out in a bedroom most of the time, just to avoid Oliver, the Supreme Kitty Kommander. We figured out too late that we'd flunked Cat Intro 101.

Experts vary on the best method, but most say that initial separation works far more often than dumping the new cat into the room and letting them sort it out.

The younger the cat, the quicker acceptance will likely take place. An adult or even teenage cat is already territorial and may be forced to fight for dominance without a gradual introduction. Established cats may not view a kitten as a threat to their territory, although welcoming a kitten warrants initial human supervision. Cats can sometimes become jealous of the newbie—whether it's a kitten or a human baby, so watch for signs of aggression in the older cats.

Smells are very important to a cat, too, and for most happy cat owners, a slow sniff under the door beats eyeball to eyeball every time. For felines who don't know or don't like each other, making eye contact is the same as saying your mother is ugly. The fur flies. Somebody gets hurt. Then you're facing a cat with injuries and perhaps a trip to the vet. Keep cats separated until the pecking order is established and the hissing dies down. Then, slowly help your kitties make friends before they merit free range of the house or catio.

Avoiding introductory disasters with our cats can teach us important lessons about how God asks us to treat our human neighbors. When we're asked to love our neighbors, we often are standoffish and try to sniff out their ways before we commit to that love.

When the new neighbor looks different or has strange ways, we often puff up our tails and arch our backs, hissing and spitting. We growl or gripe, insisting that "the other" is too this or that, thereby justifying our cattiness. We whine about motes when our eyes are loaded with logs, cross to the far side of the road, or stare at them in contempt. We ask, "Who is my neighbor?" all the while hoping God agrees with our preferences.

Of course, God wants us to avoid this kind of cat-astrophe. Maybe that's why the second half of the command says to love our neighbor *as we love ourselves*.

We are to treat others the way we want to be treated—that old Golden Rule. Luke 6:31 says simply, "Do to others as you would have them do to you" (NIV).

Simple, but not so easy. Maybe like our kitties, we must practice treating others as we would like to be treated, slowly letting the Golden Rule become a Golden Habit. When we're tempted to act as if we're better than others, we can check ourselves and change our attitude from one of entitlement to one of gratitude.

Cats have been known to fall short in the gratitude department, lording it over everything as if every feline is better than humans are. While most cats *do* behave as if humans were created to serve them, many demonstrate their thanks in unique and creative ways.

For instance, your cat gobbles up a new brand of food, so you run to the pet store and buy six cases. Yet the next day, your cat now snubs the same stuff he scarfed yesterday. Is that gratitude? Maybe it's true: if you want real gratitude, get a dog.

Joyful, Joyful, We Adore Thee

It's a fact: cat lovers gonna have cats. Most can't survive long without at least one cat to spoil, and often a single cat attracts kitty friends who visit but never leave. Their poor humans find themselves crowded into homes overflowing with cat trees, cat window platforms, cat food dishes, cat water fountains, cat beds, and cat toys.

Privileged indoor cats convince their humans to build elaborate catios—special screened-in porches that provide sunshine and fresh air while keeping kitties safe from predators and other dangers. That way, fat cats can bask without the local riffraff invading their peaceful spa.

Cat people everywhere also buy clothing and furniture to match their kitty's coat color—the better to hide the shed fur. Even more of us wear our cat's fur like a badge of honor. True cat aficionados adorn their living spaces with all things feline: calendars, pillows, coffee mugs, or those retro clocks of the black cat with moving eyes and tail. Some humans even design their entire houses around their cats, with highways near the ceilings plus top-flight kitty condos and cat-friendly niches. In these privileged settings,

cats can choose when to descend from the clouds to mingle with the lesser creatures below. The most avid cat lovers make sure everything in the décor celebrates, adores, and darn-near worships the joy of cats.

Merrimon Crawford's Alice Annabelle is a petite bundle of total love. After losing her cat Buddha, Merri looked to adopt a young, male shorthair. Instead, she kept returning to Alice Annabelle in the shelter. Now Alice Annabelle spends her days at Merri's side and isn't even interested in squirrel watching or anything else outside. Merri is thankful for Alice Annabelle, who sits daily like a loaf by Merri's feet, next to or on top of Merri and the doggy siblings, without a care in the world.

In return for all the honors and accommodations their humans provide, cats often volunteer to be mascots, sentries, and all-around pest control for cafes, libraries, cathedrals, and more. Their presence attracts people to the good vibes and laid-back ambiance only felines can provide. If the establishment hands out bonuses of tuna fish, so much the better. Cats may be lazy, but they're not crazy.

But once you admit that *you* love cats, suddenly you're labeled crazy, nutty, bonkers, round the bend. Just because your clowder grows every time you spot a stray? Because you'd spend your life savings at the vet to help a kitty? What's so loony about fostering ninety-nine kittens that go on to loving forever homes?

What can I say?

Instead of calling you crazy, maybe more people should be thankful. For a home that makes room. For keeping more kitties sheltered and healthy. For an every-two-hour-around-the-clock feeding schedule that gives newborn kittens a chance at life.

We scoop tirelessly, serve on-demand entrees, and spend our way to the poorhouse, all simply to keep this joy overflowing and off the countertops. Many kitties live far more lavishly than we do, but to us, they're worth every penny.

With that in mind, most of us don't mind being called crazy cat ladies, kitty kooks, or feline Froot Loops. As long as our cats have cute toe beans and rank high on the floofiness scale, we're good. Our feline furbabies are pure joy on four legs, enriching our days with snuggles, snoofles, and, most of all, love. That's why, at the end of the day, we can all say, "Thank God for cats!"

Prayer

Lord, thank you for your marvelous creation and for cats, the most marvelous four-legged creatures of all.

Paws-itive Faith Steps

- Send a note or card to someone who has recently had to say goodbye to a beloved kitty.
- If you're grieving the loss of a cat, share stories and pictures with sympathetic friends. Don't be afraid to talk about your loss.
- Spy on your cat or someone else's. When they don't know you're observing them, take note of the cat as she moves. Thank God for cats' special attributes, such as soft fur, swiveling ears, and twitching tail.
- Next time you feel out of sorts, snuggle with your kitty for a quick mood boost.

GLOSSARY OF CAT LINGO

(So you and your kitty can understand one another!)

Boop

A boop, when your cat head bumps you, is a most glorious sign of affection. Boops are like big, fat hugs from God—love your neighbor and your cat so you'll get more boops in life.

Blep

A blep (rhymes with *klept*), when Kitty's cute little pink tongue pokes out, is the most adorable cat expression ever. It's like your cat stopped grooming midlick to ponder life's deeper questions.

Biscuitry

Cats show you their love when they engage in biscuitry, softly or not-so-softly kneading their claws into you until your clothing is snagged beyond repair. Be thankful!

Cat-astrophe

Any situation in which your cat once again proves that you are not the boss of him. Broken, chewed, or missing items are your cat's way to keep his servant (you) in line.

Catio

Mainly built for indoor-only cats who still hear the call of the backyard, a catio is a screened-in enclosure that allows your kitty to breathe fresh air and watch birdies safely. Especially useful in areas with significant local predators like coyotes, catios also keep your cat believing that God ordained her to rule the world from her perch on the porch.

Cattoe

A cattoe is like a doggo only without the annoying dog breath and barking. Just another name for your most exalted of pets. A cattoe helps us experience God's love with skin and fur and meows on.

Chonk

A chonky cat is not fat! Maybe big-boned or all-muscle or just a little chunky. Chonks often dismay their veterinarians, but most kitties come by their pork honestly—or at least by way of second breakfast and a guy named Temptations.

Floofy

Cats with glorious hair down to there are known as floofy. These lion-maned kitties sport magnificent tail plumes and show off wild fur that definitely isn't fluffy. No, floofiness goes way beyond fluffy—and your cat knows she's beautiful. Beautifully floofy.

Judgy

That stare you get when your cat thinks you are entirely too slow at serving him. Hell hath no fury like a kitty scorned, and you can feel his judginess in that unblinking, angry stare.

Kneady

When a cat makes biscuits, she is said to be kneady. This is not the same as needy, although your cat will argue that her kneadiness is proof that she needs treats, like right now.

Kommandments

God gave Moses the Ten Commandments, so it stands to reason that cats have their own set of rules.

In fact your cat will be happy to sing these Kitty Kommandments to you any time of night.

Kleptos

Everybody knows that one guy who steals paper clips from the office, and cats have their own version of cat burglars. Kitty kleptos say they can't help themselves as they steal your unmentionables or (horrors!) your neighbor's stuff. Cats who swipe stuff need help, and if they confess, God will probably say, "Fine. Go and take underpants no more."

Kitteh

A kitteh is a cattoe as a kitty is a cat.

For the Luvva Mike

A certain cat person's mom used to say this whenever said cat person brought home yet another stray kitten. Your significant other may exclaim, "For the luvva Mike!" when you bring home another rescue or three.

Furbabies

Cats have fur, and so many times, they're our babies too. No wonder we baby our furbabies with yummy salmon pâté pablum, rattles that look like mice, and special cribs they can snub while they nap in the box the bed came in.

Meower

A cat's voice box is one of God's wonders—cats can purr, hiss, and meow with their meower.

Meow-gi

The meow-gi are little-known cats who accompanied the three kings of the East to see baby Jesus. The meow-gi say it was their idea to bring the gifts. The magi went with gold, frankincense, and myrrh, although the cats originally suggested mice, a bird, and a lizard.

Meow-Sing

When cats sing the song of their people, it is meow-sing praises to the Most High. Your cat has an incredible vocal range, best displayed from inside the carrier on the way to see the vet. The louder the singing, the more caterwauling, as cats everywhere meow their agony over unrequited love, late feedings, or rude awakenings from naps.

Mrffs

A mrff sounds like a chirp and is a cat's way of conversing with other species such as *Humans I Like or at Least Will Tolerate*. These little chirps indicate your cat is actually carrying on a conversation with you—when you get a mrff you can be reasonably sure your cat will keep you around a while longer.

'Nip

Shorthand for demon catnip, which reduces the most dignified kitty to a slobbering mess of floofiness, rolling around drunkenly on the floor. Keep the 'nip out of children's reach.

Opera-Meowser

Many cats are accomplished opera singers. Neutered cats especially love to meow-sing about their tragic lost loves. The rest go with Gilbert and Sullivan's *The Pirates of Puss-nance*.

Owwwt

If your cat cries "Owwwt!" you can be sure he wants out or—ha, ha you'll never know if he wants in or out. Owwwt is a fun game for kitties of all ages as they wait to see how long the human will open and close the door.

Rumor has it that one cat person froze to death from standing there so long. The cat never budged an inch.

Pawsies

Also called "peets," these cats' feet can be found at the end of kitty legs. Equipped with retractable "murder mittens," pawsies hide their owner's dangerous claws until needed. Then, watch out!

Paws-itive

Cats are such optimists—perhaps that's why they're paws-itive. Positive that God loves their rejoicing, kitties seize any opportunity to make the world a more cheerful place to dominate. And they're paws-itive you'll obey after they threaten to steal your phone to order more stuff from Chewy.

Puddy-Tats

Tweety Bird from the *Loony Tunes* cartoon is always the first to catch on to Sylvester the Cat's diabolical plans. Sneaky cats are identified as puddy-tats because when the canary sings, there's trouble brewing.

Purr-haps

A silly play on words can't hide the joy cat lovers get from their feline friends. *Perhaps* becomes *purr-haps* to wring extra joy out of reading about kitties.

Snoofles

A snoofle is like a boop, but with snoofles, your cat will rub your nose instead of bumping your head. Snoofles are thought to be an aid in curing any bad mood.

Singlepawedly

Cats usually work alone. They need no help to carry out their schemes of dominating your kitchen counter or hogging your spot on the sofa. Since kitties have pawsies, not hands (that we know of!), they single pawedly run our lives and ruin the drapes too.

Undercat

No undercat has ever been proven to exist, but if there was a cat who wanted to dress like a superhero, he'd surely be Undercat. Or maybe he just likes to drag your lingerie out of your dresser drawers.

Vak-koom

The vak-koom is the Darth Vader of the feline world. This red Dirt Devil was once an angel but turned to the dark side after he sucked up all the 'nip and sold his soul to that Dyson dude. He strikes fear into the heart of kitties everywhere as he feeds on shed cat fur and roars curses. His cousin, Robot Va-room-ba, tries to make up for Vak-koom's evil by offering your kitty free Uber rides around the kitchen.

Zoomies

When cats race around the house after midnight, sounding like a herd of spooked wildebeests, fear not. It's just your cats doing their zoomies. Kitties see well in the dark but still have no need of avoiding your soft parts as they galumph across your torso in the wee hours. In fact, your cat thinks you should take up zoomies too—might firm up those squishy spots he keeps trampling.

ENDNOTES

1   Karen Weir-Jimerson, "The Real Reason Your Cat Chatters at the Window," DailyPaws, August 24, 2020, https://www.dailypaws.com/cats-kittens/behavior/common-cat-behaviors/cat-chattering.

2   Leslie A. Lyons, "Why Do Cats Purr?" *Scientific American*, last modified April 3, 2006, https://www.scientificamerican.com/article/why-do-cats-purr/.

3   Stephen Dowling, "The Complicated Truth about a Cat's Purr," BBC, July 25, 2018, https://www.bbc.com/future/article/20180724-the-complicated-truth-about-a-cats-purr.

4   Julia Albright, "What It Means When Cats Knead with Their Paws," CNN, last modified August 23, 2021, https://www.cnn.com/2021/08/23/world/why-cats-knead-with-paws-scn-partner/index.html.

5   Cathleen Connell, Mary Janevic, and Preeti Malani, "Pets Help Older Adults Cope with Health Issues, Get Active and Connect with Others, Poll Finds," University of Michigan

Institute for Healthcare Policy and Innovation, April 3, 2019, https://ihpi.umich.edu/news/pets-help-older-adults-cope-health-issues-get-active-and-connect-others-poll-finds.

6   "Sleep and Sleep Disorders," Centers for Disease Control and Prevention, last modified April 15, 2020, https://www.cdc.gov/sleep/index.html.

7   "Drowsy Driving," Centers for Disease Control and Prevention, last modified March 21, 2017, https://www.cdc.gov/sleep/index.html.

8   Brené Brown, *Atlas of the Heart: Mapping Meaningful Connection and the Language of Human Experience* (New York: Random House, 2021), 187.

ABOUT THE AUTHOR
AND ILLUSTRATOR

Linda S. Clare is the award-winning author or co-author of eight books, including her latest, *Thank God for Cats!* and *Prayers for Parents of Prodigals*. A long-time writing teacher and coach, Linda also regularly contributes to *Guideposts*, *Chicken Soup for the Soul* books, and The Addict's Mom. She lives in Oregon with her family and a bunch of cats. Contact Linda on Twitter (@Lindasclare), Facebook (Linda Clare), or her website (lindasclare.com).

Sandy Silverthorne has been writing and illustrating books for over twenty-five years. He has published more than thirty books, including his award-winning *Great Bible Adventure* children's series, which has been distributed in eight languages worldwide. Sandy has worked with such diverse clients as the Universal Studios Tour, Doubleday Publishers, World Vision, the University of Oregon, the Charlotte Hornets, and the Academy of Television Arts and Sciences. You can learn more about Sandy at sandysilverthornebooks.com.